FOLKTALES OF
HAWAI'I

HE MAU KA'AO
HAWAI'I

COLLECTED AND TRANSLATED
BY
MARY KAWENA PUKUI
WITH LAURA C. S. GREEN

ILLUSTRATIONS OF PLANTS OF THE KAʻŪ
DISTRICT BY SIG ZANE

PUBLISHED ON THE
ONE HUNDREDTH ANNIVERSARY OF
MARY KAWENA PUKUI'S BIRTH

BISHOP MUSEUM PRESS
HONOLULU

FOLKTALES OF HAWAI'I

HE MAU KA'AO HAWAI'I

◀ *This graphic device in the Contents indicates that*
both an English-language and Hawaiian-language
version of the story appear in this collection.

The photograph of Mary Kawena Pukui on
page VIII *is from the Bishop Museum.*

Bishop Museum Special Publication 87

ISBN 0-930897-43-9
Library of Congress Catalog Card No. 93-74561
Printed in the United States of America

Designed and produced by Barbara Pope Book Design

CONTENTS

Mary Kawena Pukui at age fourteen

INTRODUCTION

This book honors both the Hawaiian storytelling tradition and Mary Kawena Pukui, whose birth one hundred years ago, on April 20, 1895, we may rightly celebrate as a turning point in the history of Hawai'i. A profound devotion to Hawai'i—the people, the language, the land—characterized Pukui's entire life, and she stands alone in the history of Hawai'i for her contributions to the preservation and revitalization of Hawaiian language and culture.

Born in the rural district of Ka'ū on the island of Hawai'i, Kawena grew up in the Hawaiian culture of her mother as well as the cultural sphere of her father, an American from Salem, Massachusetts. At the time, Hawaiians had become a minority in their own islands. Foreigners had overthrown the Hawaiian Islands' last monarch and were petitioning for annexation to the United States; writers were referring to Hawaiians as a "dying people." Pressure to adopt the newcomers' ways was tremendous, but Kawena's father, Henry Nathaniel Wiggin, who spoke Hawaiian fluently, and his wife, Mary Pa'ahana Kanaka'ole Wiggin, decided to raise Kawena—their only child—to be fully bilingual and bicultural.

Kawena spent the first six years of her life with her Hawaiian grandmother, Nāli'ipō'aimoku (Pō'ai), as a *hānai* or foster child. Grandparents in Hawai'i often raised a grandchild, and Grandmother Po'ai reared Kawena as a *punahele* (favored child), entrusting her with traditional Hawaiian knowledge, customs, and beliefs. Grandmother Pō'ai, who had been a *hula* dancer in the court of Queen Emma, instilled in young Kawena a lifelong passion for her Hawaiian heritage. She taught the little girl the Hawaiian language and countless chants, *hula,* sayings, and stories. Some of the tales in this volume Kawena first heard from her grandmother.

For a fuller account of Pukui's life, see the Introduction written by Eleanor Williamson in *'Ōlelo No'eau: Hawaiian Proverbs and Poetical Sayings* (Bishop Museum Press, 1983).

After the death of her grandmother, six-year-old Kawena returned to her parents' home, where her dual education accelerated. Her mother spoke to her only in Hawaiian and her father only in English. While Mrs. Wiggin continued to teach Hawaiian traditions to her, Mr. Wiggin passed on the cultural legacy and folklore from his side of the family, ranging from Aesop's Fables to the story of Ichabod Crane and the legend of Paul Revere's ride.

Both English and Hawaiian were spoken at the little Catholic school in Ka'ū where Kawena had her first taste of classroom instruction. But during the next few years, as the Wiggin family moved from Ka'ū to Puna to Honolulu, Kawena found Hawaiian language and culture less and less respected or even tolerated. Ka'ū was remote, on the political and economic periphery of the islands, but in Honolulu the Euro-American way of life was being aggressively advocated. The Wiggin family had lived in Honolulu only a short time when Kawena—then in her early teenage years—was punished at school for speaking to a classmate in Hawaiian. She did not return to school the following term.

One who loved learning, Kawena began her self-directed studies early and never abandoned them. Barely into her teens, she began to collect the stories and traditions of her Hawaiian culture, fearful that they might be lost in the sea of change swirling through Hawai'i. She jotted down sayings and stories given to her by family and friends. Her notes became the foundation for this book and many others, as well as for precious files of chant texts and ethnographic data now preserved in the archives of Bishop Museum.

In 1910, in the Book Room of the Mission Memorial Society, a chance meeting between Kawena and a neighbor, Laura C. Green, led to a friendship that helped begin Kawena's writing career. Born to missionary parents on Maui, Laura Green had an understanding of the Hawaiian language and a keen appreciation for Hawaiian culture. She was impressed by Kawena's interests and noticed her remarkable memory and talent for expressing complex Hawaiian concepts in English. Green encouraged her young friend to record her stories. They spent many hours together, Kawena dictating her tales in Hawaiian and assisting her friend with the translations. Theirs was a long and warm friendship.

Green marveled at Kawena's abilities: "She is really wonderful with so much knowledge of Hawaiian in such a young person." She sent

Kawena's stories to her cousin, Martha Warren Beckwith, Professor of Folklore at Vassar College, in New York. Beckwith edited the stories and published them, along with material from other sources, in three small volumes: *Hawaiian Stories and Wise Sayings* (1923), *Folk-Tales from Hawaii* (1928), and *The Legend of Kawelo and Other Hawaiian Folk Tales* (1936). The stories Kawena contributed to those books were the foundation for this collection, and we are pleased to publish them in her name, acknowledging her as the principal partner in their collection, translation, and preservation.

Kawena married Kalolii Pukui in 1913, and no one knew Mrs. Pukui the storyteller better than her three daughters, two of whom were *hānai*. "We grew up being taught without realizing it," recalls Patience Nāmakauahoaokawena Wiggin Bacon, her second child. "We used to walk to town together to pay bills. We could have taken the streetcar, but on the way she would point out some tree and tell us the Hawaiian name and the English name. The next time we came, she'd play a little game for us, to see if we could remember. You learn history and lore that way."

During World War II, Pukui often gathered her children together in the living room at sundown. "We started going to bed with the chickens because we couldn't have any lights," Pat Bacon remembers. "We'd lie down on quilts, and we'd discuss the day. And then she'd go into a story of this or that until we all fell asleep." Pukui took scrupulous care to tell and record *moʻolelo* (stories) just as she had heard them. "Some people heard stories and then rewrote them in a Western sense," Pat Bacon notes. "As a result, a lot was lost. That was not my mother's style. She always said, 'I'm speaking from my own doorway and not anybody else's.' You speak only of things that you know. You don't take from elsewhere." This fidelity, which characterized all of Pukui's scholarship, makes her stories especially valuable.

The publication of her folktales was the beginning of a distinguished writing career for Pukui that would greatly enrich the field of Hawaiian scholarship. With Samuel Elbert she laid the cornerstone of Hawaiian-language studies with the publication of the *Hawaiian-English Dictionary* in 1957 and its revision, the *Hawaiian Dictionary* (1971, 1986), an extraordinary achievement that is still the standard today. The two also published *Hawaiian Grammar* (1979) and teamed with Esther Moʻokini to write *Place Names of Hawaii* (1974).

Working with other collaborators, she contributed substantially to both scholarly and public understanding of Hawaiian cultural practices and beliefs, producing such seminal works as *Native Planters in Old Hawaii, Nānā i ke Kumu (Look to the Source), The Echo of Our Song: Chants and Poems of the Hawaiians,* and *The Polynesian Family System in Ka-'u, Hawai'i.* The crowning event in her career came in 1983, three years before her death, with the publication of her treasury of Hawaiian expressions, *'Ōlelo No'eau: Hawaiian Proverbs and Poetical Sayings.* By that time Pukui was a highly sought-after *kumu* (source or teacher) of Hawaiian knowledge. She was held in high esteem as a cultural expert, a translator, a genealogist, a *kumu hula,* and a teacher and lecturer. For more than five decades she worked with Bishop Museum—translating, compiling research, and conducting anthropological field work. She entrusted her knowledge to be a part of the legacy preserved and shared by the museum.

In old Hawai'i, storytellers were accorded a position of honor. Storytelling served as a principal source of entertainment while simultaneously providing instruction in the many interwoven aspects of life—ancestry, history, religion, human relations, crafts, and the natural world. Throughout her life, Pukui was an ardent practitioner of the art of storytelling. She told stories to everyone—to schoolchildren, to researchers and visitors at Bishop Museum, and, above all, to her family and friends. She knew the importance *mo'olelo* held in old Hawai'i and recognized their importance in conveying information and values that remain meaningful and necessary for people in Hawai'i today, whether of Polynesian ancestry or not.

Unfortunately, we cannot receive these stories as Pukui's daughters and Laura Green did—in her own voice. Most folklore is better heard than read, since much is lost in the transfer from oral telling to the written word. While taking down these stories from Kawena, Laura Green lamented the inadequacy of writing to convey what she was hearing: "I wish an instrument was in my possession," she wrote in a letter to Martha Beckwith, "to take the intonations of her sweet Hawaiian voice—boast, scorn, humility, anger—that the stories might be reproduced thus."

Though nuances of the oral tradition have escaped, this book furnishes the next best thing to a live telling, presenting many of the tales in Pukui's original Hawaiian as well as in her English translation. Gifted Hawaiian speakers may be able to restore some of the missing emotional shading by taking cues from Pukui's choice and arrangement of Hawaiian words. Unfortunately, a number of the stories were originally published solely in English and without explanation; it is not known if the Hawaiian-language versions still exist.

These stories were set down long before it became standard practice to use 'okina to indicate glottal stops or kahakō to designate long vowels. Readers of Pukui's day could satisfactorily discern the intended pronunciation and meaning of a word from its context, but most Hawaiian-language authorities today employ 'okina and kahakō, and we have followed that practice. (There are a few exceptions, for example, the Pukui name is printed without an 'okina between the two final vowels because Mrs. Pukui preferred to remain faithful to the spelling that her husband's family used, and under which she always published.)

M. Puakea Nogelmeier, the first recipient of the Mary Kawena Pukui Scholarship at the University of Hawai'i at Mānoa, and now a Hawaiian-language instructor at the university, generously assisted in reviewing the manuscript and standardizing the Hawaiian spelling. He also organized the stories in a sequence that reflects the order of traditional hula presentations, placing stories of the gods first, followed by those of chiefs, and then tales of ordinary people.

Some of the English phrasing in the tales has been edited slightly for a modern audience, but care has been taken to retain the cadence of Pukui's original English. Footnotes have been added or amended to clarify references and explain matters of context. New footnotes are designated "Ed." (editor), those written by Martha Beckwith carry her initials, and the remainder are from Laura Green or Pukui.

The stories in this collection range across a broad spectrum of subjects and styles. They are full of veiled and double meanings. Readers are invited to interpret these texts for themselves, but it is important to remember that these *mo'olelo* are part of the culture that engendered them, and the more one learns about that culture, the more alive the stories become.

Pukui's was, at times, a lonely road. Pat Bacon recalls that some people objected to her efforts, questioning her right to interpret Hawaiian culture, while others resented the recognition she came to receive. "Writing gave her great pleasure," her daughter says, "but a lot of heartache went into it. People would rant and rail at her. When she was doing the dictionary, people would call her up and curse her. She would come back in tears. But she kept at it. She'd tell us, 'If I don't do it, who's going to?'"

Mary Kawena Pukui gathered and told the stories that appear here out of a deep devotion to Hawaiian culture, a love her family instilled in her as a child and to which she devoted her entire life. She and her ancestors are perpetuated in these *mo'olelo*.

W. Donald Duckworth
President and Director, Bishop Museum
Honolulu, Hawai'i
1995

Wauke

THE LEGEND OF NĪ'AUEPO'O

Hina was the mother of Nī'auepo'o, Kūalakai the father.[1] Kū came from Kahikinui'āle'ale'a to Māniania in Ka'ū and lived with Hina. At length he said to his wife, "I am going back to Kahiki'āle'ale'a from whence I came. When our child is born, if he asks for me, give him these tokens by which I may know him—my red helmet, my red feather cape, and my canoe with red sails. Send him to me in this canoe and in this only."[2]

Hina's son was born and named Nī'auepo'o. As he grew up, he noticed that the other boys had fathers, and he asked Hina where his own father might be. "Alas! He is dead; only we two are left," she told him. He persisted in asking, and at length she told him of his father in Kahiki and showed him the tokens. When he refused to go in his father's canoe, she went to consult her parents about the boy's wish to travel to the land of his father. They advised her to call upon their ancestor Niuolahiki to conduct the boy and gave him two gifts, an arrow and a bow, to take with him to Kahiki. In the morning at daybreak Hina called upon her divine ancestor:

> *E Niuolahiki*
> *I kupu i Kahiki,*
> *I mole i Kahiki,*
> *I kumu i Kahiki,*
> *I lau i Kahiki,*
> *I hua i Kahiki*
> *I o'o i Kahiki ē!*

> O life-giving coconut
> That budded in Kahiki
> That rooted in Kahiki
> That formed a trunk in Kahiki
> That bore leaves in Kahiki
> That bore fruit in Kahiki
> That ripened in Kahiki![3]

Instantly, a coconut sprouted from the ground in front of her door and grew into a tree with two coconuts upon it, in which she recognized her ancestor. Waking her son, she told him to sit among the leaves of the tree

1

and hold on tight and not to fear. The boy took his bow and arrow, seated himself among the leaves, and held tight. Higher and higher grew the tree until the leaves looked like a mere dot in the sky.[4] The boy was frightened and called to his mother, "O Hina! Hina! My hands and feet are numb with fear!"[5]

Hina called back, "O life-giving coconut, hold your grandchild fast!"[6] Then the boy lost his fear through the *mana* of the divine ancestor.

There was now no land in sight. Higher and higher grew the tree, and again fear gripped the boy. He called, "O Hina! Hina! My hands and feet are numb with fear!"

Hina, anxiously listening, heard the voice of her son faintly and called back, "O life-giving coconut, hold fast to your grandchild!"

Up and up they went; then at last the tree bent over toward Kahiki-'āle'ale'a. In alarm the boy cried out, "O Hina! Hina! My hands and feet are numb with fear. I am losing my grip and shall fall!"[7]

Very faintly came the words to Hina's ears, and she called back, "O life-giving coconut, take care of my son!"

Ever downward bent the tree until its leaves rested on the land of Kahikinui'āle'ale'a. Then, assuming human form, the ancestor said to the boy, "Guard well your grandparents' gifts; the arrow will lead you wherever you wish to go."

Nī'auepo'o walked along the shore until he came upon a group of boys who were playing and shouting. "Who are you and where do you come from?" they cried.

"I am Nī'auepo'o and I live in this neighborhood," he replied.

"No, you do not," a few retorted. "We live hereabouts ourselves, and we have never seen you before."

"Come and join us in our play," invited others. So Nī'auepo'o became one of the merry, shouting boys.

Someone proposed a contest of skill, and they fell to work to make a large mound of sand to mark a course for surfing. They paddled out on their boards to meet the surf and turned shoreward, each trying to keep in line with the mound they had built. Those who kept in line surfed again and again. Those who missed went ashore to watch the others. The game continued until Nī'auepo'o alone was left the victor. So it was with every game proposed—boxing, spear-throwing, footraces, *'ulu maika* (bowling)—Nī'auepo'o excelled in all.

One of the boys in the group, named Uhuʻula, admired his skill and asked Nīʻauepoʻo to become his friend, and the two boys strolled away together. Nīʻauepoʻo now remembered his arrow, and he sent it flying, along with the words, "Cry 'nē!' over the bald-head, 'nē!' over the drooping-lidded, 'nē!' over the one-eyed, 'nē!' over the hunchback, and lead me to the place where I belong!"

The arrow sped on, whistling over the bald-head, the drooping-lidded, the one-eyed, and flying over the head of a hunchbacked woman who stood outside of a large grass house. It entered the door of the house, where a young girl caught it quickly, rolled it in a piece of fine *kapa,* and held it firmly in her hand. She looked up as the shadow of the two boys in the doorway fell across the mats.

"Have you seen my arrow?"

"No, I have not seen it."

"I saw it come in here."

"Perhaps you are mistaken; there is no arrow here."

"Let me call it, and it will answer."

"Call it, then."

So, Nīʻauepoʻo called, "O arrow of my grandfather, where are you?"

"Here!" answered the arrow.

"Come to me!"

The arrow moved to obey, but the girl held on tight, hoping that the boys would enter the house after the arrow, and finally she invited them to do so. As soon as they were inside, the hunchback, at a sign from her mistress, closed the door, and the girl took Nīʻauepoʻo for her husband.[8]

Now, the girl was the daughter of Kūalakai by another wife, one who lived here in Kahikikū, and the chief had promised himself that when his son came from Hawaiʻi, this girl was to become his son's wife, and he had set two old men to watch at the beach for the coming of the canoe with the red sail. When he heard that the girl had already taken a husband, he was very angry, and proceeding to the house of the girl and addressing Nīʻauepoʻo, he asked, "Who are you?"

"I am Nīʻauepoʻo, son of Hina and Kūalakai."

"If you are indeed Nīʻauepoʻo, where are the red helmet, the red feather cape for your shoulders, the canoe with the red sail, and my sacred canoe?"

"Those I left with my mother in Hawaiʻi."

"You are an imposter and shall die, both you and your friend here!" The two boys were seized and bound, and when the *imu* was prepared, they were killed and baked therein.

That night a great rainstorm swept over the land, washing away leaves, stones, charcoal, bodies, and all, washing them out of the *imu* into the sea. There Niuolahiki in his eel form took charge of the bodies of the boys and carried them to the gods of the sea, where they came to life again, Nī'auepo'o in human form and Uhu'ula in the form of a red fish.

Three nights later, the two guards watching at the shore for Nī'auepo'o to arrive by canoe saw a handsome youth rise out of the sea and come to the shore. Observing a fine paved walk leading to a well-built house by the shore, he called, "O Kahikiloa! O Kahikipoko! For whom was this walk made?" And they both answered, "For Nī'auepo'o."

"First they kill Nī'auepo'o, and then they say that the walk is made for him!" And stepping boldly upon the walk, he went toward them.

Seeing the bathing pool beside the house, he said, "O Kahikiloa! O Kahikipoko! Whose bathing pool is this?"

"It is for Nī'auepo'o."

"They have killed Nī'auepo'o, and yet they say that this is his bathing pool!" Plunging into the water, the youth bathed in the pool. Pointing then to a loincloth suspended from the overhanging bough of a tree, he said, "O Kahikiloa! O Kahikipoko! Whose loincloth is this?"

"It is for Nī'auepo'o."

"They have killed Nī'auepo'o, and yet they say that this is his loincloth!" And he wound the cloth about his loins.

At the door of the house, he paused and said, "O Kahikiloa! O Kahikipoko! Whose water gourd is this?"

"It is for Nī'auepo'o."

"They have killed Nī'auepo'o, and yet they say that this is his water gourd!" And he drank from the gourd.

"O Kahikiloa! O Kahikipoko! Whose drum is this?"

"It is for Nī'auepo'o."

"They have killed Nī'auepo'o, and yet they say the drum is for Nī'auepo'o!" And he sat down and continued drumming upon it until it grew late.

"O Kahikiloa! O Kahikipoko! Whose sleeping mats are these?"

"They are for Nīʻauepoʻo."

"They have killed Nīʻauepoʻo, and yet they say that these mats are for Nīʻauepoʻo!" And he lay down on the mats.

"O Kahikiloa! O Kahikipoko! Whose sleeping *kapa* are these?"

"They are for Nīʻauepoʻo."

"They have killed Nīʻauepoʻo, and yet they say that these *kapa* are for him!" And he drew the *kapa* over himself.

"Wake me early, O Kahikiloa and Kahikipoko, that I may depart before the sun is warm." In the morning they wakened him early, and he went away into the sea.[9]

For four nights, the father of Nīʻauepoʻo heard the sound of his son's drum and was uneasy. He called the watchkeepers and heard the story from them. Then he summoned two prophets and asked them to see what being it was who came up each night out of the sea and beat upon his son's drum, drank from his son's gourd, slept upon his son's sleeping mats, and covered himself with his son's sleeping *kapa*.

The prophets prayed and declared to him that it was no other than his own son, who had come on the back of his ancestor Niuolahiki to seek his father. In order first to appease the ancestor, he must prepare gifts of a pure black pig a fathom in length, black ʻawa drink, a red and a white fish, and take them to the sea and call upon Niuolahiki. If he was willing to forgive the chief, he would arise in his eel body and eat the offering; then he would not fight against him when the chief endeavored to catch his son. Next, instructed the prophets, when his son had come up into the house, he should take ten long nets and surround the house and then offer to him exactly the same food which had been given to his ancestor, without varying it a bit. If he varied it, there would be trouble.

The chief sent men to carry out the prophets' charge. The ancestor rose from the sea and ate the offering. At night the nets were laid, and the chief and his men hid in the sand before the youth appeared.

After the sun was set, the boy came up out of the sea, and as his feet touched the land, he called, "O Kahikiloa! O Kahikipoko! I see eyes, bright eyes, staring at me out of the sand!"

"Those are crabs, just sand crabs! Only we two are here."

"O Kahikiloa! O Kahikipoko! Whose paved walk is this?"

"It is for Nīʻauepoʻo."

"First they kill Nī'auepo'o, and now they say it is for Nī'auepo'o!"

The father listened and heard the questions and answers repeated for the bathing pool, the loincloth, the water gourd, the drum, the sleeping mats, and the sleeping *kapa*. The two old men then questioned the youth, and he told them all he knew about his parentage, his journey to Kahiki, and what had happened since his coming. In the meantime, the chief drew near and listened to the story and knew that this was indeed his son Nī'auepo'o.

The sun was high the next day before the men awakened Nī'auepo'o. The youth dashed out of the house and found himself caught in a net. He tore through it and felt another net about him. As he neared the last net, they brought the girl whom Nī'auepo'o had made his wife and placed her within it. She held him with her arms until the men had succeeded in covering both with the net and taking them into the house, where the food was laid before Nī'auepo'o with prayer. He ate and became as he was before he was killed. All desire to fling himself into the sea left him, and on the sixth day, he and his half-sister went away to her home to live together. The chief, however, had observed that the red fish had by some mistake been omitted in the offering and knew that trouble was in store for him.

In the meantime, in Ka'ū, Hina knew that evil had befallen her son, and in answer to her prayer, her shark guardian appeared and carried her over the sea to Kahiki'āle'ale'a. There she fought her son's father for killing her son and threw him into the sea, where the gods of the sea in pity turned him into the first *kūalakai* fish.

Hina then returned to Ka'ū and married again, and her first child, a daughter, she named Māniania, Numb, in memory of the brother's sensations when he went over the sea with his ancestor Niuolahiki. The place where Hina lived in Ka'ū district is still called Māniania, after the daughter who was born to her there.

This story is a variant of the Oʻahu legend of Kalanimanuia (Fornander, Bishop Museum Memoirs 4:548–550), whose name is related to the place-name in this Hawaiian legend.

1. *Kūalakai* means Kū road (of the) sea. The boy's name, Nīʻauepoʻo, is problematic. *Nīʻau* is the stem of a coconut leaf, but the etymology of the last syllables is doubtful. *Eʻe* means to climb upon, and *poʻo* means head.

2. The parents Kū and Hina and the recognition tokens are standard elements in tales of marriages which take place during the visits of a chief on his travels.

3. This invocation is employed by medicinal herb gatherers as a prayer to Kū and Hina, the patrons of medicine. See *American Anthropologist* 28:202 (1926).

4. The stretching tree as a means of passage to the land of a stranger parent is found in the Kauaʻi romance of the chiefess Laukiamanuikahiki (ibid. 4:596–598). The preparations made by the chief for receiving his child and the child's appropriation of them also are found in other sources.

5. *E Hina ē! E Hina! Māniania mai nei oʻu mau lima me oʻu mau wāwae!*

6. *E Niuolahiki ē! Paʻa ʻia, paʻa ʻia kō moʻopuna.*

7. *ʻAneʻane au e hemo a e hāʻule!*

8. The arrow incident is also in the Hawaiian story "Hiku and Kawelu" (Fornander, Bishop Museum Memoirs 5:182).

9. Handy says, in relation to similar accounts in Marquesas stories of the preparations made for a first-born son, that it is the custom for a Marquesan chief to plant fruit trees and paper mulberry, stock a place with pigs, and build a bathing basin in readiness for the use of his first-born. See *Marquesan Legends*, Bishop Museum Bulletin 69:61 note.

THE BREADFRUIT TREE

The god Kū, who was of a polygamous nature, once came to Hawai'i and married a Hawaiian woman, with whom he lived many years and raised a large family. He did not tell the woman that he was a god; he worked on the land like anybody else.

A time came when food was scarce and no one could get enough to eat. Kū's wife and children were starving. Kū was sorry for them. He told his wife that he could get food for them by going on a long journey but that he could never return to them. At first, his wife would not hear of it, but she finally consented to his going when she heard the children crying with hunger. Kū said, "Let us go into the yard." There he said good-bye to the woman and told her that he was going to stand on his head and disappear into the earth. Then she must wait until his toes appeared out of the ground. Out of them would grow food for the family. He stood on his head and began to sink into the ground; first his head and shoulders, then finally his whole body disappeared.

His wife watched the spot every day and watered it with her tears. One day a sprout appeared, and from it a tree grew so rapidly that in a few days the family had the food that Kū had promised. It was the breadfruit. The wife and children ate all they wanted. Only they could pick the fruit; if anyone else tried, the tree would run back into the ground. After a time, sprouts grew about the parent tree, and these were given to friends and neighbors to plant in their own gardens. Thus Kū's gift blessed his people.

This story, as here written by Laura C. S. Green, has been handed down from father to son as long as the Hawaiians have lived in the islands. It is supposed to have originated either in Sāmoa or Tahiti, and to have come with the breadfruit tree when it was introduced into Hawai'i.

The Hawaiians have another story attributing the tree to Haumea. The low-lying breadfruit is called *kino o Haumea*, "body of Haumea," and *nā 'ulu hua i ka hāpapa*, "low-lying like a bush." It is thought of as female. The ordinary upright tree is called male and named *'ulu kū*, or "upright breadfruit."

According to Rock, only one species of breadfruit, the *Artocarpus incisa*, is known in Hawai'i, although others are well known in the southern island groups (*Indigenous Trees of the Hawaiian Islands*, 115–117). Since this species is propagated only through suckers and not through seeds, it must have been brought to Hawai'i by migrants from another island group.

'Ulu

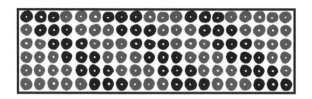

KĀNE AND KŪ

This is a legend told about a certain old man who lived in Hilo (on Hawai'i) in very ancient times.[1] He was a man who never doubted his gods, Kāne and Kū.[2] Upon arising in the morning, he would say, "O Kāne, listen! O Kū, listen! I have arisen." When he was preparing a meal, he would say, "O Kāne ! O Kū! I am preparing my food." When it was cooked, he invited them thus: "O Kāne! O Kū! The food is ready and I am to eat; come and eat with me!" When his appetite was satisfied, he would exclaim, "O Kāne, listen! O Kū, listen! I have had enough." When he fetched his digging stick[3] to till his sweet potato patch, he again called to his gods, "O Kāne! O Kū! I am going to dig; let us go together!" In this way he called constantly upon his gods in everything he did.

One day he went with some friends to the seashore for fish. His net caught upon a piece of sharp coral in the ocean. He called upon Kāne and Kū, saying, "I am going to dive to free the net!" and down he dived forthwith. His friends waited for him to rise to the surface, but as he did not appear, they thought he was dead and took word to his family to this effect.

When the old man dived, the coral and net vanished, and he found himself in a beautiful country. He said, "O Kāne! O Kū! This is indeed a wonderful land! I will seek the inhabitants of this country."

As he walked along, he saw a grass hut and heard a voice calling him. Joyfully, he hastened forward, exclaiming, "O Kāne! O Kū! One of the inhabitants is calling me, and I am going to him!"

Arriving at the hut, he saw two old men. He was entertained graciously and slept there that night. In the morning, one of the old men said to him, "Look here! We are constantly hearing you call our names. I am Kāne, this is Kū. It is really respectful of you not to invoke us on those occasions when you are relieving yourself. But you utter our names so continually on all sorts of occasions that we have grown weary. That is

11

why we have brought you here, to teach you [what is proper]. Remember us when you rise, call upon us in trouble, and when you lie down to sleep, meditate upon us. Now go, and when the right time arrives, we will come for you."

They sent the man back to his own home. His relatives and friends were happy to see his face again and to hear about the beautiful land he had seen. Many years after, he disappeared, and it was said he had gone to live with his gods, with Kāne and Kū.

The Hawaiian-language version of this story, *Kāne a me Kū,* appears on page 106. This story was related in Hawaiian by Lily Akuna, a cousin of Mary Kawena Pukui.

1. This is a humorous folk rendering of the curious story of Makuakaumana, a fine version of which appears in Rice's *Hawaiian Legends,* pages 116–132.

2. Two of the four great gods of Hawai'i.

3. 'Ō'ō, a hardwood stick from three to four feet long, sharpened into a slanting point at one end, which farmers used to dig while sitting in a crouching position. The modern spade-shaped digging implement used in Hawai'i today is called by the same name.

THE WILIWILI TREES OF PĀʻULA

There were four daughters born to their mother—Moholani the first-born, next Wiliwiliʻoheʻohe, then Wiliwilipeʻapeʻa, and last of all Wili-wilikuapuʻu.[1] Moholani was the most beautiful of them, for the beauty of Wiliwiliʻoheʻohe was marred by baldness, and Wiliwilipeʻapeʻa had a mass of tangled hair which tossed here and there when the wind blew. As for Wiliwilikuapuʻu, the hunchbacked one, we can see from her name that she lacked beauty altogether.

Moholani was the only one who was married. She had one child, named Kauilamākēhāokalani, which means "Lightning flashing from the heavens." This son was given into the care of the gods to be brought up in Kuaihelani, the land hidden in the clouds.[2]

Moholani's husband often went to a point on the seashore, where he was seen and admired for his vigorous bearing by certain women *kupua* of the sea. They endeavored to ensnare him. ʻAhikananā was the name of one of these women and ʻAhikāhuli of the other. They seized every opportunity to tempt him by chanting the songs of the sea and relating tales of the deep blue ocean. Finally, bewitched by their wiles, he plunged into the sea and accompanied them to their cavern at the ocean floor.[3]

After waiting long for her husband to return, Moholani went in search of him to every place she knew, and those who had seen him told her of his being ensnared by the enchantresses. So as she neared the spot where her sisters lived, she called, "O Wiliwiliʻoheʻohe, listen! Come to my aid! O Wiliwiliʻoheʻohe, come to my aid! Do you know if my husband has been carried away by ʻAhikananā and ʻAhikāhuli to the place where the little stones rattle?"

But Wiliwiliʻoheʻohe looked at her crossly and answered, "Ugh! He is a big, worthless man! I do not know where your husband is!"

Moholani walked on, weeping, to the second sister and called, "O Wiliwilipeʻapeʻa, listen! Come forth! O Wiliwilipeʻapeʻa, come forth! Do you know if my husband has been carried away by ʻAhikananā and ʻAhikāhuli to the place where the little stones rattle?"

But Wiliwilipeʻapeʻa answered like her older sister, "Ugh! He is a big, worthless man! I do not know where your husband is!"

Moholani went on to the home of her youngest sister and cried out the same words, but she got no different answer than from her other sisters, for Wiliwilikuapu'u said, "Ugh! He is a big, worthless man! I do not know where your husband is!"

Now, Moholani, perceiving that she was to get no sympathy from her sisters, sought her son, requesting the gods who were his foster parents to allow him to leave them. Kauila, upon hearing his mother's lament, went forth to seek his father.

When 'Ahikananā and 'Ahikāhuli refused to relinquish their lover, the boy's wrath flashed forth; because of their obstinacy, he changed his body into a lightning flame, and at the glancing of this lightning on the ocean floor, the women were cut into pieces and transformed so that from them come all that kind of fish called mackerel. Gone forever was their power to tempt other women's husbands, for they were now nothing but fishes!

Because of their unkindness to Moholani, the three sisters were transformed into *wiliwili* trees.[4] Because Wiliwili'ohe'ohe was bald, she became a tree which is almost leafless; Wiliwilipe'ape'a became a tree whose leaves flutter in the whispering breeze; and as Wiliwilikuapu'u was a hunchback, her trunk became crooked.[5]

As for Moholani's husband, he refrained from wandering again, for he realized that he had a son whose anger, once aroused, could not be assuaged.

The Hawaiian-language version of this story, *Nā Wiliwili o Pā'ula*, appears on page 107. This story was told by Mrs. Wiggin in Hawaiian and dictated to Miss Green by her daughter, Mary Kawena Pukui.

1. These names suggest certain mental associations: *Moholani* means heavenly champion. Her younger sisters take their names from a native tree *(Erythrina sandwicensis)*, with the various suffixes describing their appearance. *Kuapu'u* means hunchback. [Ed.]

2. One of the twelve hidden islands of Kāne.

3. Compare Thrum's story of the siren woman in "Punaaikoae," *More Hawaiian Folktales*, pages 85–196. [M.W.B.]

4. These trees are said still to be standing on the beach at Pā'ula.

5. The appearance of a *wiliwili* tree actually varies according to its environment and the weather. It has, says Miss Green, "all the characteristics borne by the sisters." *Wiliwili* wood is buoyant, and Hawaiians use it for the outriggers of canoes.

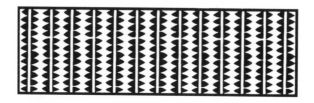

ANELIKE, THE ROLLING SWEET POTATO ISLAND

'Ualaka'a, or Rolling Sweet Potato, was one of the twelve hidden islands of Kāne, and it was ruled over by Kānekokai, Kāne Who Owns the Sea. This Kāne had twelve daughters, of whom the eldest, named Anelike, and the youngest were the prettiest. The youngest had been adopted in her infancy by Kānekokai and was considered so sacred that no mortal could ever set eyes upon her except in times of trouble.

When Anelike grew to womanhood, a great desire possessed her to visit the land of Hawai'i. So, diving into the sea from a high, potato-shaped cliff, she swam and swam until she reached her destination. There a handsome fisherman named Kanakaokai, or Man of the Sea, after the mighty sea-god of that name, found her sitting alone on the sand, and he took her home to his parents and gave a feast in honor of this strange maid of the sea. After a while, he asked her to become his wife and she readily consented. A strange wife indeed for a fisherman, for she scorned all food except *pi'oi* or *lama* berries![1]

In those days, there was not much food for people except fish and mollusks and a few berries, for Makali'i had tied everything up in a huge net and hung it in the sky.[2]

Anelike soon tired of living with human beings. She grew peevish and fretful, and found fault with her husband. This resulted in a quarrel, after which she swam back to the land of her birth.

Day after day, Kanakaokai awaited her return. He walked from beach to beach, hoping against hope to catch a glimpse of her. Early one morning, he saw a woman swimming toward him and ran to the spot where she was likely to land. His wife had come!

But instead, this woman was a total stranger. "Aloha!" she called.

"Aloha!" he answered.

"Alas, grandson!" she said, "I have come because of your tears for Anelike. I am her grandmother, and I alone can tell you how to reach her."

15

"How?" he asked eagerly.

"Swim out to sea. When you see a rock covered with 'ākulikuli, the scarlet-flowered purslane, that is the highest peak of Moku'ākulikuli, the Island of Silence, one of Kāne's islands, which is about to appear from the depths of the sea.[3] Don't stop! Swim on until you see a black, barren rock, which is Moku'ele, Black Island. Keep right on until you come to a potato-shaped rock. Grasp it and rest; there you will find your wife."

Kanakaokai waited for no further instructions. Away he swam to search for his bride. About an hour's swim took him to Moku'ākulikuli, the Island of Silence. Another hour took him to Moku'ele, Black Island, and after the third hour, he reached the rock shaped like a potato. Weary and hungry, he climbed to safety and was soon wrapped in slumber. He dreamed of the good woman of the sea who had directed him hither. "Kanakaokai," she seemed to say, "Anelike is still angry with you and plans to kill you. Ten fair maidens will come, one after another, claiming to be Anelike. Be sure to make every one angry. When the eleventh comes, neither answer nor look up, for it will be Anelike herself. If you answer, she will smite you; but be silent until she pities you, and then she will give you a forgiving kiss."

Kanakaokai awoke and found himself on the summit of a mountain, for the island had come up to the surface of the sea. Slowly, he descended to the valley below.

In the meantime, Anelike's sisters had seen and admired him. They told Anelike how they had found him asleep on the mountain. But she answered, "Go and see, each for herself, if you can attract him. I surely hate him enough to kill him!"

So one sister started off to try her charms upon him. Drawing near to Kanakaokai, she called, "O Kanakaokai, listen! Here am I, Anelike!" He turned to look at her and answered, "You are not Anelike; your beauty can reach only to the neck of Anelike!"[4] She was angry and returned to report her failure to her sisters. The next one tried, and she too came back angry; she had been compared to Anelike's back.

One by one, Kanakaokai compared the sisters to various parts of Anelike's body—the arm, thigh, knee, leg, ankle, toes, and soles of her feet. Tearfully, they reproached her for sending them. "Go yourself," they sobbed, "and see how you like being insulted! He called us legs, heels, ankles, thighs. We were never called such names before."

Anelike reached for her best *pāʻū*, wrapped it about her waist, and went forth to see her husband.⁵ When she came in sight of him, she called, "Here am I, Anelike, your wife!" He kept his head bent to the ground and did not answer. "Kanakaokai! Look up! Can you not hear me calling you?" Still he made no response. Again and again she called and he remained silent, until at last her pity was stirred, and she kissed him on his forehead. Looking up, he smiled upon his long-lost wife.

He was by this time very hungry, and grasping a stick of sugarcane, he began to chew it; next, he ate a few bananas. Anelike looked on in surprise, for no one on her island ever ate such things, and she had never seen anyone on Hawaiʻi eat anything but berries, fish, and mollusks. "Oh, Kanakaokai!" she cried, "you will make yourself ill. Eat the *piʻoi* and *lama* berries, for we have plenty of those here."

"Rats' food, birds' food! Indeed, I have seen the birds pecking at them and the rats eating them with relish. So I turn to the food for which they care little!"

"Rats' food?" thought Anelike. "Indeed, I must learn to like human food better." Then she sat beside him and shared his sugarcane.

"Alas!" cried her sisters, who had now come to seek her, "you will poison yourself! Let us eat too that we may all die together!" Their cries brought their attendants, who also wept bitterly.

Kāne himself heard these sounds of lamentation and sent his adopted daughter mounted on the back of a huge dog.⁶ She spoke to them as follows: "Sisters and relatives of my sisters, weep not! These things are not poisonous. Eat, Kanakaokai! Bake the roots of the taro and potato. Someday soon an insignificant little creature will scatter food throughout the islands, and all men shall eat freely of fruit and vegetables."

At these words, their grief was soon turned to joy. And a few months afterward, a mouse nibbled open the huge net of Makaliʻi, and food then grew plentifully all over the islands.

This story was told by Mrs. Wiggin and dictated to Miss Green by Mary Kawena Pukui.

Rice has published a fine version of this story in *Hawaiian Legends*, 19–31. There are touches in this fairy tale that suggest modern innovations, but the theme is well known in Māori legend, where the lost mistress is sought in the heavens instead of under the sea. We get here a picture of those habitable islands lying on the sea bottom that Māui and other fishing heroes drew up to the surface to form the Polynesian archipelagoes. In Hawaiian mythology, Kāne is believed to own "twelve mysterious islands," which appear and disappear at his will. On one of these islands is found the "water of life of Kāne." Mrs. Pukui names six, as follows: 'Ualaka'a, Moku'ākulikuli, Kānehunamoku, Kuaihelani, Paliuli, and Moku'ele. Good souls go to Kānehunamoku, "Hidden island of Kāne." In *Fornander Collection*, 5:678, the breadfruit is said to have come from this island. See also page 532 of the same volume for the origin of the name *'Ualaka'a*. [M.W.B.]

1. *Pi'oi* is perhaps the ancient name of *lama* berries [*Diospyros* spp.], which are found in Ka'ū and in other dry sections of the islands and were probably plentiful in the old days. The plant grows, says Mrs. Wiggin, "from four to five feet in height" with "leaves something like a cherry's." It has yellow fruit "shaped like small peppers."

2. According to legend, in ancient times a greedy chief named Makali'i used his supernatural powers to gather all the food plants into a great net and then to suspend it in the heavens. [Ed.]

3. *'Ākulikuli* is a general name for many kinds of succulent plants. In modern usage, *'ākulikuli* usually refers to sea purslane, *Sesurium portulacastrum*.

4. For the test of beauty by means of such itemized comparisons, see *Laieikawai*, chapter 2: Fornander's story of Kepaka'ili'ula, whose uncles go out to search for a girl pretty enough for him to marry; and Fornander's tale of Kalanimanuia, whose ghost body recovers the different parts of his human form and wins in a beauty contest for the sister's hand. Compare also the treatment of this theme in the Indian story noted in volume 2 of Penzer's edition of Tawney's translation of Somadeva's *Katha-sarasagara*. [M.W.B.]

5. The *pā'ū* was the principal garment of a Hawaiian woman in former times, consisting of barkcloth wound about the waist and hanging to the knee. The supernatural power of a woman often resides in this garment; hence, in the stories it becomes one of the gifts bestowed by a supernatural woman ancestor upon the favorites of fortune. Shaking it can create storm and devastation. In both "Laieikawai" and "Aukelenuiaiku," it is by shaking the *pā'ū* that the goddess raises a storm to destroy her enemies. [M.W.B.]

6. In the Fornander legend of Wahanui (*Fornander Collection* 4:518), the island of Kānehunamoku attacks certain voyagers in the form of a savage dog. Compare *Laieikawai*, composed by Hale'ole, chapter 17. [M.W.B.]

KŪKAʻŌHIʻAAKALAKA

Kūkaʻōhiʻaakalaka, Kū the ʻŌhiʻa of the Forest, was the brother, and Kauakuahine, the Sister Rain, was the sister. They came from Kahiki and lived in Hawaiʻi, the sister in ʻŌlaʻa with her husband, and the brother at Keaʻau with his wife. The brother had no children, the sister had a flock of them. Her husband was a farmer in ʻŌlaʻa, the brother a fisherman in Keaʻau.

The sister often brought vegetables to the shore for her brother and returned with fish for her family. The brother told his wife to give his sister an abundance of dried fish when she came with the vegetables. The wife hated to give up the fish and laid it under the sleeping mats. While the husband was out fishing, the sister came with vegetables and the wife said, "We have no fish, as you can see for yourself; all we have is salt." The sister went and gathered coarse seaweed to take the place of fish. Again she came with vegetables and went back without anything. She was lucky to get the seaweed. This constant stinginess of her sister-in-law vexed the sister. It seemed to her useless to burden herself with carrying vegetables and to return with only seaweed for her patient husband and children. One day when she came close to the house and her husband and children ran out to meet her, she gave them each a slap and changed them into rats, the husband into a large rat and the children into young rats. She herself became a spring of water where fine rain fell.

While the brother was out fishing, the gods showed him how stingy his wife had been and how his sister had become a spring and her family had changed into rats. He was much distressed and returned home and asked his wife, "Did you give fish to our dear sister?"

"Yes, I always give her fish."

He saw the dried fish laid flat beneath the sleeping mats and what a heap of them there were. He was very angry with his wife. "What a cruel woman you are! You have brought misfortune upon our little sister!"

And with many words of reproach, he beat his wife to death.

He ascended to his sister's place in 'Ōla'a and saw the rats scampering about where the house had stood, and he shed tears of love for his brother-in-law and the children. He went straight to the spring, plunged in headlong, and was changed into an *'ōhi'a* tree.

This tree bears only two blossoms to this day, and when a branch is broken off, blood flows from the body of the tree.

The Hawaiian-language version of this story, *Kūka'ōhi'aakalaka,* appears on page 111. This story was told to Mary Kawena Pukui in Hilo, Hawai'i, 1930.

Kūka'ōhi'alaka is one of the gods worshiped by those who go up into the forest to hew out canoes or timber for building (Malo, *Hawaiian Antiquities,* 113, 169). His image in the form of a feather god is worshiped at the time of building a *heiau,* together with Kūnui-ākea, Lono, Kāne, and Kanaloa (Fornander, Memoirs 6:14). His name is given as the father of Kaulu by his wife Hinaulu'ōhi'a at Kailua in Ko'olau district on O'ahu (Fornander, Memoirs 4:522; 5:364).

Emerson says that *laka (rata)* is the name of the *'ōhi'a* or *lehua* tree in Tahiti, Raro-tonga, and New Zealand (Malo, 115–116, note 5).

THE ROCK OF HANALEI AND THE ROCK OF LĒKIA

When Pele and her immediate family came from Tahiti, certain rock *kupua* accompanied her to the islands of Hawai'i, namely Rock of Hanalei, Rock of Lēkia, Rock of Kua, Rock of Mālei,[1] Rock of Ka'a, Rock of Kāne,[2] Long Rock, and Rock of Lono. Rock of Hanalei lived at Hanalei, Kaua'i; Rock of Lēkia lived in Kapoho, Puna; Rock of Kua and Rock of Lono both dwelt in Ka'ū, Hawai'i. Long Rock lived for a time in 'Ōla'a, Hawai'i, but later moved to the island of O'ahu. Another one of the group who lived on O'ahu was Rock of Mālei, at Makapu'u. Rock of Ka'a was a rolling rock, going wherever he willed; therefore, one cannot clearly state where his home was. And Rock of Kāne made his home in Kona. This story is concerned with Rock of Hanalei and Rock of Lēkia.

When Pele came to live permanently in the mountains of Hawai'i, her heart ached for Rock of Hanalei, who was still living on Kaua'i. Pele sent for her to become one of her household at Moku'āweoweo, and Rock of Hanalei accepted the invitation.

Sometimes they all went down to Puna for bathing in the sea, sledding, and other pastimes of the old days.[3] Rock of Lēkia always accompanied these pleasure parties. He was carried away with the beauty of Rock of Hanalei and asked Pele if he might win her as his wife. Pele, seeing how fond they were of each other, consented.

After the marriage, the couple returned to the place which Rock of Lēkia had chosen for their home. There they stand on the hill to this day. The story about them and the *kupua* Kālaikini is well known to all the old inhabitants of Puna district.

The Hawaiian-language version of this story, entitled *Ka Mo'olelo o Pōhakuohanalei a me Pōhakuolēkia*, appears on page 113. This story was related by "old lady Kanaloa" of Pāhoa, Puna, and dictated by Mary Kawena Pukui.

1. In the story of Pā'ao, Mālei is called a hunchbacked female *kupua* who accompanied Pā'ao to Hawai'i. The Pele family is supposed to have come to Hawai'i during the same period as the migration of Pā'ao. [M.W.B.]

2. Compare Rice, *Hawaiian Legends,* 32.

3. The sledding was done on the long, slippery grass of a smooth hillside.

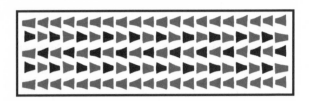

THE STORY OF PĀ'ULA

This is an ancient story of Pele which takes place in the Ka'ū district, between Nā'ālehu and Honoapu.

Pā'ula was a beautiful woman who lived on the beach of Pā'ula. She had two friends almost as beautiful as she. All were fond of the game of *kimo,* and the spot where they loved to play was called Kalaeokimo, that is, the Cape of Kimo.[1]

Pele had a lover whom she adored and endeavored to keep entertained with music, but he soon wearied of that and wandered off one afternoon bent on pleasure. He met Pā'ula tossing her pebbles and counting them while her companions were swimming in the sea. He sat down before her and challenged her to a game, and for three days and nights they played, pausing only long enough to eat.

But Pele missed and sought him. When she found him with Pā'ula absorbed in a game of *kimo,* in rage she smote them both and turned them into two headless masses of rock. There they are still to be seen, sitting facing each other with the pebbles between.[2]

Down at the point of the cape, two friends of Pā'ula were found playing at *kimo,* and they too were smitten. But no trace of them remains—only the pebbles they were tossing.

This story was told by Mrs. Wiggin.

1. The Hawaiian game of *kimo* is much the same as jacks but is played with small stones. In Tahiti and New Zealand the game is also played with pebbles, while in Fiji and Sāmoa a variety of mimosa bean is used. [M.W.B.]

2. Pele's jealousy is commemorated in this fashion about the coast of Hawai'i. Between Kahauale'a, where stands the *heiau* of Waha'ula, and the blow-hole called Puhi o Kālaikini after the local sorcerer of that name, at low tide one may see the rock body and breast of Halaaniani, whom Pele also transformed out of spite "because she was too beautiful." It is at this place on the Puna coast that anything thrown into the water will come ashore at Ka'ū, and I believe this reflects a love affair in which messages were exchanged, Tristan and Isolde fashion, by lovers in the two districts. [M.W.B.]

THE BREADFRUIT OFFERING

Two girls who were roasting breadfruit in the upland plain boasted of their gods. "Laka is my god, a beneficent god!" said one.

"Kapo is my god, an amiable god!" said her companion.[1]

While they were thus praising their gods, an old woman appeared. She said to the first girl, "Give me some of your breadfruit."

"No," answered the girl, "my breadfruit belongs to Laka."

"Is Laka a powerful god?"

"Yes, a powerful god indeed!"

"Give me some water from your gourd."

"No, indeed! This water belongs to Laka."

The old woman turned to the second girl and asked her for breadfruit. Knowing that she had not vowed the breadfruit to her favorite god, she gave it gladly. When the old woman had eaten, she asked for water from her gourd and received it. When she rose to go, before leaving she said to the girl who had treated her kindly, "Go home and tell your parents to store food in their house and to hang up flags for ten days at the corners of the house."

When the girl told her family what the old woman had said, they knew that it was no old woman, but Pele herself. They were glad that the girl had been kind to her. They obeyed all her commands, and when ten days had passed, fire from the volcano appeared above Mokuʻāweoweo. The lava flowed over Kaʻū district and destroyed many homes but spared the house and family of the kind-hearted girl.

Parents and grandparents teach their offspring not to be stingy, not to answer strangers rudely, that they might not offend Pele someday and have evil befall them.

The Hawaiian-language version of this story, *Ka Mōhai ʻUlu*, appears on page 114. Mrs. Lifte of Kahaluʻu, North Kona, Hawaiʻi, told the same story of two girls at Puʻuhuʻehuʻe.

1. Laka and Kapo are sisters of Pele, goddess of the volcano.

THE GOD OF LOVE

Makanikeoe, the god of love, had two sisters named Lauka'ie'ie and Laukiele'ula, Leaf of the Vine and Leaf of the Red Blossom.

Lauka'ie'ie was the eldest. She helped her brother and sister, for she had supernatural power superior to theirs. She never married, but went about doing everybody good. It was she who made the wild plants grow. She had a wonderful cowrie shell called Kaleho'ula, which had the power to carry her wherever she desired to be.

Lauka'ie'ie was so beloved by the gods that when the time came for her to put aside her human body, she became the clinging 'ie'ie vine, beneath whose protecting leaves the choicest *maile* is to be found. To this day, when the natives go in search of *maile*, they look for the spot where this 'ie'ie vine grows best.

As for Laukiele'ula, she had authority over fish of every sort; even the shellfish came at her call. She was the wife of Moanalīhauokawaokele and mother of Kahalaomāpuana, the sweet-smelling pandanus. Later, Laukiele'ula was changed into a fragrant, blossoming plant.[1]

The love-god himself assumed the form of a tree, whose branches made pretty, tinkling sounds when the wind blew. If anyone broke off a branch, a loud voice called, "Now you give back my limb! Who gave you the right to take it?" If the person restored the branch to the tree, there would be no further annoyance, but anyone who ran away with a branch would hear the call for ten days and ten nights. If someone still persisted in retaining the branch, the god would appear in a dream or vision and bestow a blessing. Thus, the person would become a powerful love-sorcerer and have the power to make any people he pleased love each other.

The following story is told of how the god of love befriended the man Kānekoa and restored his wife to him.

1. In the romance "Laieikawai," as composed by Hale'ole, the daughter goes to visit her parents in the heavens. In Fornander's romance "Kaulanapokii," the same heroine appears under another name and by means of her magic arts causes vines to grow up and imprison the enemies upon whom she wishes to avenge herself. All the plants mentioned in this story—'ie'ie (a stiff, woody vine of the forest), *maile*, the pandanus blossom or *hala*, the red *kiele* with its sweet perfume, and the plants later summoned by the god of love—all are considered especially sacred to the god and are used in decorating the temple and the dancers for religious ceremonies. [M.W.B.]

'Ie'ie

MAKANIKEOE, THE GOD OF LOVE

It is said that Makanikeoe and his sister Lauka'ie'ie came to the district of Puna from foreign lands. Upon their arrival, they said to each other, "You go your way and I will go mine."

Makanikeoe spied the mouth of a certain cave and, entering, followed along a secret passage and came out on the side of a mountain, where he found a man weeping.

Through his power as a god, he recognized the man as Kānekoa and asked him, "What are you doing here?"

"I am here because my father and my mother-in-law have cast me out and taken away my wife," answered Kānekoa.

The god could not help laughing. "What caused all this trouble?" he inquired.

"My mother-in-law thinks me an idle, worthless person," said Kānekoa. "She is not satisfied unless I am always working. If I rest while I am cultivating the land, she calls it laziness; if I stop awhile when out fishing, that is idleness also. She wants me to work without ceasing."

The god invited Kānekoa to share his cave, saying, "You are to become a good friend of mine and you must give attention to all that I teach you."

As they approached the cave, there appeared spontaneously bananas, 'awa, taro, sweet potatoes, and yams through the power of the god.

Then the god told Kānekoa, "Pound an abundant supply of taro root, then go to the side of the road and invite wayfarers to partake." Kānekoa did as he was told; he pounded the taro root for food and called to the travelers, "Come and eat! Come and eat!" Those who were hungry followed him to the cave and ate, and they took back to Ka'ū this strange news about Kānekoa.

About this time, Kānekoa's father and mother-in-law began to enter into negotiations with another man who wanted to marry their daughter.

When they heard the news about Kānekoa, they were so indignant that they immediately set out for 'Ōla'a with the man whom they had chosen for their new son-in-law, intending to kill Kānekoa.

The god, who knew of their plan, warned his friend. "I am going to change myself into a tree and stand at the mouth of the cave," he said. "When your wife's relatives come to do you harm, step on my body." This was the first intimation Kānekoa had of his friend's divinity.

Kānekoa went to the roadside as usual, and presently he saw his wife's relatives approaching. While his mother-in-law scolded him, his rival ran forward with a wooden club intending to kill him.

Kānekoa ran to the entrance of the cave and climbed upon a limb of the tree. Instantly, he felt himself being gently lowered. The trunk of the tree became like the body of a man, and a loud voice cried, "Hearken, O tree ferns!" and the ferns cried, "Here we are! Here we are!" He called to the bird's-nest fern and the fiber-bearing vine and to every wild plant of the mountain, to other ferns, also to the mountain-apple tree and the *maile* vine, and each responded, "Here we are! Here we are!"

The terror-stricken intruders threw down their clubs and fled, imagining that they had heard the voices of the innumerable gods of the wilderness.

Soon after this, the god, knowing that a famine was to come upon the district of Ka'ū, directed his friend, "If your wife comes to ask for food, feed her, but drive off her relatives and friends; surely, since they have called you an idle, worthless fellow, they cannot eat your food!"

"If they come weeping I may pity them," said Kānekoa.

"Drive them away and see what will happen," insisted the god.

When the famine came as had been predicted, many came to Kānekoa for food and, returning, reported to the people of Ka'ū, "Kānekoa has an abundance of food." His wife went weeping to her mother and said, "It is because you have driven away my husband, the only one who has a food supply, and because you want me to take this new husband—that is why we now feel the pangs of hunger.

So the family set out for the cave. Kānekoa, fearing to disobey the god, allowed only his wife to enter; the others waited without. When they tried to enter, the magic tree hit them with its branches and drove them away.

After a little, the wife said to her mother, "I have a vision of the feast of Kānekoa. Let me go away to the seashore day by day to seek black crabs for food."

"Go child, for we are weak with hunger," replied the mother.

Then the wife flew to her husband, and when her appetite was appeased, she returned to her mother, saying, "There were no black crabs at all on the shore!" This she did day after day until she grew quite plump and pretty, while her parents were starving with hunger.

At last the parents could endure it no longer. They begged Kānekoa to take pity on them, calling him "our good son and provider of parents." The god forgave them and promised them food, only they must return to Kānekoa his wife and banish the new husband, and then go home to their own home and leave the wife to live with her husband. Kānekoa pitied his starving rival and gave him sweet potatoes before he went, but the father and mother-in-law stoned him out of the district and he took refuge in Kona.

After this, the god bequeathed to his friend the cave and all its provisions and went forward on his mission of love. Once, according to the story, he found a woman with a broken leg and carried her back to the cave and gave her to his friend to care for, bidding him treat her kindly as he himself had been treated.

To this day, when there is quarreling in the family, old Hawaiians in Ka'ū remark, "Makanikeoe is gone from home," and when peace is restored they say, "Makanikeoe has returned."

The Hawaiian-language version of this story, entitled *Makanikeoe, ke Akua o ke Aloha*, appears on page 115.

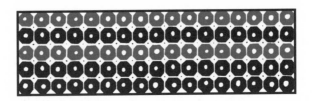

WOMAN OF THE FIRE AND WOMAN OF THE WATER

There were two *kupua* women living in Hilo on the island of Hawai'i. Hinaikeahi, Woman of the Fire, was the elder, and Hinaikawai, Woman of the Water, was her younger sister. To the elder belonged the power to work magic with fire; to the younger, similar powers with water. Each was given her portion of land and retainers by her mother Hina.[1]

Once, famine came and there was great lamentation among the people because of hunger, and many infants died because their mothers could not provide them with milk.[2]

As Hinaikeahi saw her people's distress, her compassion flowed out to them and she called them all to gather before her. Then she commanded the men to be strong and to climb the mountain after fuel and bring stones from the river in order to prepare an underground oven, or *imu*. When everything was brought, she ordered them to prepare a very hot oven. Amazement filled the men's hearts at the command to prepare an oven when there was no food to be cooked, but out of love for their chiefess, they did it all without a murmur.

When the oven was ready, Hinaikeahi circled it, saying as she did so, "Here are sweet potatoes, here taro, here yam, dog, pork, fish, the tender shoots of young fern, and here chicken!" Then she walked into the center of the oven and called to her retainers to cover her with earth.

The men wailed, "No! no!" Hinaikeahi spoke thus: "O my people, do not weep, but cover me over with earth. And I will go to our divine ancestors that you may have life. Watch, and on the third day you will see a cloud directly over this oven in the form of a woman with a radiant face. Then remove the earth. Now cover me!"[3]

With great reluctance, the men did as their beloved chiefess commanded them. On the third day, a cloud in the shape of a woman appeared directly over the oven, and immediately the men uncovered it. There was no body lying there, but the foods she had enumerated were there—yam, taro, fish, and all the rest. And after the oven had been opened, Hinaikeahi appeared, coming from the direction of the seacoast and wreathed with brown seaweed. In haste the food was served, and all were seated at the feast while Hinaikeahi related the story of visiting her divine ancestors, who had shown their love for her by providing this feast. After the ancestors had filled the *imu,* she had bathed in the ocean with Hinaʻōpūhalakoʻa, the Woman of the Coral, who was one of the wives of the god Kū.⁴

According to the custom of society, this incident caused much talk, and the retainers of Hinaikeahi boasted about the delicious food their mistress provided. The followers of Hinaikawai therefore complained to her, reporting what they had heard from her sister's retainers. Thus, the spirit of jealousy entered Hinaikawai, and she commanded her retainers also to prepare a great oven, and when this was done, she imitated her older sister by repeating the names of various foods and then calling upon her retainers to cover her with earth.

The third day, the sky was overcast and a dark cloud in the form of a woman stood directly over the *imu.* The men made haste to remove the covering. Alas! No food was visible—only the charred body of Hinaikawai. Rain began to fall after the oven was opened, and it was said that this was the weeping of heaven for Hinaikawai. If she had only used her own gift of water, she would have been saved, but instead she was jealous and flew to usurp the magical gift of her older sister; hence, the penalty for her pride. When her retainers saw that they had neither chiefess nor food, they all went to live with Hinaikeahi.

The Hawaiian-language version of this story, *Hinaikeahi a me Hinaikawai,* appears on page 118. This story was told to Mary Kawena Pukui when she was a child by an old lady from Hilo, Hawaiʻi, named Kanui Kaikaina.

1. Hina is the consort of the god Kū and *wahine* is the generic name for woman or wife. There are many Hinas in Hawaiian tales and genealogies, just as Kū has many manifestations.

2. In ancient days, the mother's milk was the only means of nourishing a young child; hence, a ritual was employed at birth to ensure milk to the mother and another at the time of weaning the child.

3. Compare with the garbled story of the breadfruit tree in *Fornander Collection* 5:676. The idea of a god's burial to provide some form of food for his people is a common convention in Hawaiian storytelling, familiar also in the South Seas. [M.W.B.]

THE BEAUTIFUL KEAMALU

Keamalu, or Clear Shade, lived in Paliuli, that wonderful land where Lā'ieikawai dwelt.[1] She was brought up as carefully as Lā'ieikawai. Birds guarded her and fed her with *lama, pi'oi,* and *māmaki* berries, and with the honey of *lehua* blossoms.[2] She did not eat ordinary food; she was brought up on the food of birds.

A spring in the mountains of 'Ōla'a is called Pūnāwai o Keamalu, Spring of Clear Shade, and there Keamalu went to bathe. One day as she sat by the spring, a young man appeared to her and asked her to become his wife. She refused, for she did not want to marry, and when he insisted, the birds came and took the girl away on their wings. The young man returned to Puna, to his sweetheart Kalehua'ula, the Red Lehua Blossom. While his body remained in Puna with that handsome woman, his thoughts were in the uplands of 'Ōla'a. Again and again he visited the uplands, finding no rest for his passion. Not finding Keamalu, he went back to Kalehua'ula. Keamalu remained hidden in the house for fear of meeting the young man.

The parents of Kalehua'ula heard how he was running after Keamalu, and they asked him teasingly, "Is the girl really so beautiful?"

"Yes, she is really beautiful," replied the young man.

"Our daughter is indeed beautifully formed. How can that common girl of the forest be compared to our daughter?" Now it was true that Kalehua'ula was beautiful, but her eyes were sullen.

Keamalu remained hidden until she thought that the young man had forgotten her; then she returned to the spring. But she was seized by the youth and released only when the hawk had scratched his face and arms. Then the birds carried her away once more. Keamalu's guardian *kupua* heard of the slighting remarks made by the parents of Kalehua'ula, and they determined to have a test of beauty between their child and the beauty of Puna.[3] They sent a messenger to her parents, who accepted without hesitation, for their daughter was famous for her beauty all over Puna. They did not know that her opponent was the foster child of the *kupua* of Paliuli. Thus it was decided; Keamalu was to pick her flowers and place them inside a certain big gourd, and Kalehua'ula was to place her flowers inside a gourd, and the gourd over which the birds hovered would be the winner.

When the day came for the contest, the Puna girl put pandanus blossoms and red *lehua* into her gourd; Keamalu filled hers with *maile* vine and white *lehua*. 'I'iwi hung over Keamalu's flowers, while only a fly flew over those of Kalehua'ula.[4] The parents were angry and insisted that the girls themselves should be compared. This was just what the foster parents wanted. Everyone was invited to come on that day and witness the great contest. When Kalehua'ula appeared, all praised her beauty, but when Keamalu was brought forward by her foster parents, the people saw that she was more lovely than anyone they had ever seen. They struggled for places to see this incomparable beauty. The parents of Kalehua-'ula turned away in shame. The young man's proposal for Keamalu was accepted, and the two were married and lived happily in the uplands of Paliuli.

As for the spring of Keamalu, it was hidden and is shown to very few people.

The Hawaiian-language version of this story, *Ka U'i Keamalu,* appears on page 120.

1. A mythical earthly paradise, sometimes identified with one of the twelve islands of Kāne but in Hawaiian romance placed on the island of Hawai'i, in the wooded uplands of 'Ōla'a between Puna and Hilo districts.

2. The berries of the *lama* (*Maba* spp.) [*Diospyros* spp.] are, according to Rock, reddish yellow when mature and are eaten by people as well as by birds. The botanical identification of the *pi'oi* is uncertain, but it may be an upland vine with clusters of light yellow berries, which are eaten by the natives. The *māmaki* is the genus *Pipturus*, from which Hawaiian barkcloth is commonly made.

3. For the beauty match, compare with the story of Kalanimanuia, Fornander, Bishop Museum Memoirs 4:548–552.

4. The '*i'iwi* (*Vestiaria coccinea*) is a honeysucker and insect eater which makes its home in the high uplands, where its scarlet color may be seen and its sweet casual note heard among the flowering *lehua* trees. It is the most highly colored of all Hawaiian birds.

THE MAGIC PIPES

Kauakahiali'i was a ruling chief of Pihanakalani, a sacred valley on Kaua'i.[1] His parents died when he was an infant, and he was adopted by Kahalelehua,[2] a *kupua*[3] who could be, at will, a woman or a huge *'ōhi'a* tree covered with scarlet blossoms.[4] She guarded her adopted son so well that if any human being was curious to see him, she would fill her valley with the thickest of mists and gather him up into her flower-laden boughs. No human being ever attended him; she and her retinue of *kupua* guarded him day and night.

As he grew to manhood, she taught him to play on two magic pipes— Kanikawā, a loud-sounding one, and Kanikawī, a shrill one. When he attained manhood, he heard among his attendants whisperings of the beauty of Ka'ililauokekoa, chiefess of Maka'iwa, near Kōloa, Kaua'i. So when he had a chance, he climbed up the mountainside during the darkness of night and piped this song:

> *Kani ka pū i Pihanakalani,*
> *E Ka'ili, e Ka'ili, e Ka'ililauokekoa, ē!*
> *Ua moe 'oe!*
> *Hāli'ali'a mai ana kō aloha ia'u,*
> *E Ka'ili, e Ka'ili, e Ka'ililauokekoa, ē!*
> *Ua moe 'oe!*
> *Moe ana 'oe, a ho'olōlō ana*
> *I ke kani o ka 'ohe o Kanikawī,*
> *E Ka'ili, e Ka'ili, e Ka'ililauokekoa, ē!*
> *Ua moe paha 'oe!*
> *Eia me a'u kou aloha a hiki i ka mole o Lehua,*
> *E Ka'ili, e Ka'ili, e Ka'ililauokekoa, ē!*
> *Ua moe 'oe!*

I sound the pipe here on the ridge of the mountain,
O Ka'ili, O Ka'ili, O crescent leaf of the *koa* tree,
    You sleep.

Little by little I draw your love toward me,
O Ka'ili, O Ka'ili, O crescent leaf of the *koa* tree,
    You sleep.

34

Koa

Sleeping you stir and listen
To the song of the pipe called "Shrill voice."
O Kaʻili, O Kaʻili, O crescent leaf of the *koa* tree,
  Do you feign sleep?

Your love is mine, firm as the bedrock of Hawaiʻi.[5]
O Kaʻili, O Kaʻili, O crescent leaf of the *koa* tree,
  You sleep.

The young man was lonely and piped to please himself, with no idea that his words could be carried over the cliff to Makaʻiwa, but such was the magic of the pipes that they could convey the words themselves as well as the sound of the music.[6]

For five nights, Kaʻililauokekoa heard the sound of the piping; on the fifth night, she awoke her attendant,[7] and together they searched for its source. All night long, they clambered over the cliff. At dawn the music ceased, and the girls found themselves at the entrance of the sacred valley.

Its supernatural guardians, seeing the beauty of the chiefess, allowed her to enter, but for three days and three nights Kahalelehua held her adopted son captive in the boughs of her tree form. Kaʻililauokekoa sought everywhere but could find no lover. On the third day, the *kupua* resumed her human shape and released her captive. He and the girl stood and gazed at each other, but soon they made friends, and Kahalelehua, seeing how well matched they were, sent word to the girl's father that she desired to keep her for a daughter-in-law.

For three months, everyone prepared for the marriage. New cloth was beaten and perfumed,[8] mats woven,[9] and food-stuffs brought for the feast. On the day of the marriage, lightning flashed, peals of thunder were heard, and the land was covered with mist, all these signs proclaiming the royal blood of the young couple.

A few months after the marriage, Kaʻililauokekoa said to her husband, "I shall soon fall into a deep sleep; do not bury me and do not mourn for me." It had been a custom of the girl from her childhood to sleep for months at a time.[10]

The day arrived and she fell asleep; she ceased to breathe. For twelve months her husband guarded her, but at the end of that time, he lost his courage, fearing she would never awaken. He therefore tucked the pipe

Kanikawā into her bosom, called upon her supernatural guardians to take care of her body, and taking Kanikawī, he traveled from island to island to drown his grief.

After two years of travel, he came to the home of Waka, a relative of his foster mother, who was the supernatural guardian of Lāʻieikawai.[11] Day by day he watched this beautiful chiefess who reminded him so vividly of his wife. After a time, Waka asked him to become the husband of her ward, and he consented to a long engagement.

Now one day a stranger accompanied by a young companion came to the home of Lāʻieikawai. At every assembly, for amusement, this stranger would tell the story of Kauakahialiʻi and Kaʻililauokekoa.

Kauakahialiʻi asked her name and birthplace, but she merely shook her head. He said, "You remind me of my wife!—are you my wife?" She smiled and repeated the story. He began to dog her steps; where she went he followed. One morning early, he entered her house while she was fast asleep. He touched her chest and there felt a hard object. He drew it out and found that he held in his hand his own pipe, Kanikawā. Drawing Kanikawī from the belt of his loincloth, he piped his song:[12]

> I sound the pipe here on the ridge of the mountain,
> O Kaʻili, O Kaʻili, O crescent leaf of the *koa* tree,
> > You sleep.

The stranger awoke and wept.

A few days later, he went to Lāʻieikawai and asked her to release him from their engagement, telling her the joyful news that he had found his wife. He and Kaʻililauokekoa returned to Kauaʻi.

Afterward, he sent his friend Kekalukaluokēwā to Hawaiʻi to seek Lāʻieikawai as wife. The adventures of that journey are to be found in the romance of Lāʻieikawai.[13]

Compare with the Māori version in Grey's "Hine-moa, the Maiden of Roturua," *Polynesian Mythology* (Auckland, 1885), 146–152. Hawaiian versions of the story have been published locally in *Hawaiian Annual*, 1907; *Paradise of the Pacific*, 1911; and Rice, *Hawaiian Legends*, 1923. The story resembles that of the displaced bride in European fairy-tales. [M.W.B.]

1. An allusion to the frequent mists that obscure the valley Pihanakalani, a sacred valley above Hanalei, the northern district of the island of Kauaʻi.

2. Kahalelehua, the Tree House, alludes to the tree body of the *kupua*. Compare with Fornander's story of Hoamakeikekula, 4:532–538.

3. *Kupua* is the name applied to a demigod, who has the power of changing form.

4. *ʻŌhiʻa (Metrosideros polymorpha)* has a flower sacred to the gods because of its brilliant scarlet color. It is used to decorate the altar at the *hula* ceremonial. The timber trees of the same genus grow to a great height and form the great forests which cover the slopes of the mountain below the volcano in the districts of Puna and Hilo, on Hawaiʻi. Their fine-grained timber is valued for cabinetwork.

5. *A hiki i ka mole o Lehua;* lit., "reaching to the taproot of Lehua island." [Ed.]

6. *Pali*, cliff or precipice.

7. Malo says, "The person who brought up an *alii* (chief) and was his guardian was called a *kahu*." (page 85).

8. *Kapa*, or *tapa*, Hawaiian cloth made by pounding into a mat the fibrous inner bark of certain plants. To perfume a *kapa*, the powder from the blossom of the male *hala* (pandanus) tree was sprinkled in the bottom of a calabash and the *kapa* placed in it and covered, airtight, for several days. The leaves of the *maile* vine *(Alyxia)*, dried and crushed, serve the same purpose. See Malo, *Hawaiian Antiquities*, chapter 16; Brigham, *Ka Hana Tapa*, Memoirs of the Bishop Museum 3:165.

9. *Moena*, mats, woven from the prepared leaves of certain plants.

10. Compare the magic sleep in the story of ʻŌpelemoemoe, "Opele the Sleeper," *Fornander Collection* 5:168–170. [M.W.B.]

11. The account of this episode in the life of the beautiful chiefess of Puna appears in chapter 3 of the romance by Haleʻole (translated in the 33d *Annual Report of the Bureau of Ethnology*, 368–370). In this version, Kauakahialiʻi travels about the islands to find someone as beautiful as Kaʻililauokekoa (whose magic sleep is not explained in the story). His friend makes an appointment for him with Lāʻieikawai, who promises that the notes of certain birds will herald her approach to the dwelling of the chief. The first time, she is coy and disappoints her lover; when she appears the next night, the wife, Kaʻililauokekoa, is there before her. [M.W.B.]

12. *Malo*, girded about the waist and between the thighs.

13. The episode of how Kekalukaluokēwā courted the beauty of Puna appears in chapter 19 and following of the romance by Haleʻole. Kauakahialiʻi, dying, wills to his friend the magic flute Kanikawī, which can win for him whatever he desires, and bids him go to Puna and wed Lāʻieikawai. That in this case the magic flute eventually fails of its mission is probably the fault of interpolaters and not of the original version of the story. [M.W.B.]

THE STORY OF MIKOLOLOU

Mikololou was a shark from the Kaʻū district on the island of Hawaiʻi. One day, he and his shark friends Kua, Kealiʻikauaokaʻū, Pākaiea, and Kalani set out on a visit to Oʻahu. On the way, they fell in with other sharks all going in the same direction.

Arriving at Puʻuloa, which is the place now called Long Hill off Pearl Harbor, they encountered Kaʻahupāhau, the female shark who guarded the entrance of Pearl Harbor. She had another body in the form of a net extremely difficult to tear, with which she captured all alien sharks who entered her harbor. Her brother Kahiʻukā, the Smiting Tail, struck at intruders with his tail, one side of which was larger than the other and very sharp.[1] These two and their followers were not man-eating sharks, and the people on land guarded them well, taking them food and scraping their backs free of the barnacles that attached themselves there.

When the visitors arrived, one of them remarked, "Ah! What delicious-looking crabs you have here!"[2] Now, man-eating sharks speak of men as "crabs," and Kaʻahupāhau knew at once that some of the strangers were man-eaters. But she could not distinguish between the good and the bad sharks, hence she changed into the form of a great net and hemmed in her visitors while the fishermen who answered her signal came to destroy them.[3]

Kealiʻikauaokaʻū changed himself into a *paoʻo* fish, which lives among the rocks, and leapt out of the net. Kua changed into a *lupe*, as the spotted stingray is called, and weighed down the net on one side, helping his son Kalani and nephew Pākaiea, who were half human, to escape. But before anything more could be done, the fishermen hauled in the nets they had brought to land, and poor Mikololou was cast upon the shore with the evildoers, where they were left to die of the intense heat.

All were soon dead but Mikololou. Though his body died, his head lived on, and as the fishermen passed to and from their work, his eyes followed them and tears rolled down his face. At last his tongue fell out. Some children who were playing nearby picked it up and cast it into the sea.

Now Mikololou's spirit had passed out of his head into his tongue, and as soon as he felt the water again, he became a whole shark.[4] With a triumphant flop of his tail, he headed for home to rejoin his friends. When Ka'ahupāhau saw him, it was too late to prevent his departure.

I ola 'o Mikololou i ke alelo, "Mikololou lived through his tongue," is today a saying among the Hawaiians, implying that, however much trouble one may have, there is always a way of escape.

Ka'ahupāhau no longer lives at Pu'uloa, coming and going at will with her twin sons Kūpīpī and Kūmaninini. But when the United States government built a drydock for the Navy just over the old home of Ka'ahupāhau, the natives regarded the proceedings with superstitious fear. Scarcely was it completed when, after years of labor, the structure fell with a crash.[5] Today, a floating dock is employed. Engineers say that there seem to be tremors of the earth at this point, which prevent any structure from resting upon the bottom, but Hawaiians believe that the Smiting Tail still guards the blue lagoon at Pearl Harbor.

As told by Mrs. Wiggin. For an almost identical version of this story, see Thrum, *More Hawaiian Folktales,* Chicago, 1923, page 307. Emerson (see "Hawaiian Shark Aumakua," in *American Anthropologist* 19:512 (1917) makes Mikololou's home at Pōkini, Mōlīlele pali, Ka'ū, according to a note collected March 16, 1907, from W. P. Kāneali'i. [M.W.B.]

1. In *Papers of the Hawaiian Historical Society,* no. 2, page 10, Mr. Joseph Emerson gives a pleasant picture of "Kaahupahau and her brother Kahiuka, the two famous shark-gods of the Ewa lagoon on this island. Their birth and childhood differed in no essential features from that of other Hawaiian children up to the time when, leaving the home of their parents, they wandered away one day and mysteriously disappeared. After a fruitless search, their parents were informed that the children had been transformed into sharks. As such, they became the special object of worship for the people of the districts of Ewa and Waianae, with whom they maintained the pleasantest relations, and were henceforth regarded as their friends and benefactors." In Emerson's version, Mikololou is represented as a man-eater. He is lured up the Waipahu River and feasted with 'awa until he can easily be snared in nets and dragged up on shore, whence he escapes, as in Thrum's version. Ka'ahupāhau was supposed to be dead when Emerson wrote (in 1892), but Kahi'ukā still lived in the old cave by the sea. His last keeper, Kimona, sometimes found his fishnets missing and knew that Kahi'ukā had carried them upshore to a place of safety. [M.W.B.]

2. When the man-eating shark of Maui, Pehu, is lying in wait for a surfer at Waikīkī

and is asked what he wants, he answers, "I am catching a crab for my breakfast!" See Thrum, page 304; Westervelt, *Legends of Old Honolulu,* 56. [M.W.B.]

3. Compare the old Hawaiian saying, "Alahula 'o Pu'uloa, he alahele na Ka'ahupāhau." [Also compare Mary Kawena Pukui, *'Ōlelo No'eau: Hawaiian Proverbs and Poetical Sayings,* page 14. Ed.] In Thrum's version, the nets are spread by the fishermen. The sharks tear through four, but the fifth is too strong for them. The number of nets probably corresponds to the ritual number five in the worship of the god Kū. [M.W.B.]

4. In Thrum's version, a dog swallows the tongue. A little later, the dog jumps into the sea for a swim and is transformed into the shark Mikololou. [M.W.B.]

5. This happened about 1914. The government bore the cost of the failure and no blame was attached to the company who built the dock, but whether the old shark-gods entered into the case I have never heard reported. [M.W.B.]

BLOSSOMS OF PĀ'ULA

Nāpuaopā'ula, Blossoms of Pā'ula, was a very pretty girl of Pā'ula in Ka'ū district. Many praised her beauty, and she became a great favorite with her family. Close to her home lived a household that was jealous of her because she was praised for her beauty, and their own child was homely.

Between Pā'ula Beach and Kahaoa lived a shark *'aumakua* of these jealous people.[1] Every day they went with *'awa,* bananas, and other good things to feed the shark. They first poured the *'awa* into the shark's hole, and when the shark's head appeared, they fed it the food they had brought. Because of their jealousy of Nāpuaopā'ula, they commanded the shark to take her life.

Nāpuaopā'ula was returning with her parents from planting, and as she went close to the beach, they saw a swelling wave shaped like a white chicken rise and dash over the girl. The parents heard a wailing cry and saw their daughter being cruelly handled by the shark. He dragged her from Kahaoa to Kawanui and from Kawanui back to Kahaoa. The girl cried to her parents, "O my parents! I am dying. Love to you!"

The broken-hearted parents consulted a *kahuna* as to the reason their beloved child had met with this misfortune. The *kahuna* told them that the shark was the *'aumakua* of the people living close to them and said that if they loved their daughter, they would bring him a black pig, a white cock, and black *'awa*.[2] All these commands they fulfilled. Not long after, the mother became pregnant and bore a daughter. They named her Nāpuaopā'ula. She was the exact image of her sister.

As for those evil-minded people, they contracted a swelling disease and died. First the father contracted the disease and died, and then the wife died. Thus all the members of the family died; there was not one left. Nāpuaopā'ula the younger and her parents moved away from the place. No one fed the evil shark any more, and it was neglected in every way. For this reason, that shark hole was greatly feared because it was known that a man-eating shark lived there.

The Hawaiian-language version of this story, *Nāpuaopā'ula,* appears on page 122.

1. An *'aumakua* is a family guardian, half-god, half-human, whose worship is handed down from generation to generation. An *'aumakua* may appear in the form of various animals or objects, but the cult of the shark *'aumakua* is well-nigh universal for persons living along the sea.

2. The offering laid before the priest is one given to the *kahuna 'anā'anā or kahuna ho'opiopio* for the service of praying an enemy to death. See J. S. Emerson, Haw. Hist. Soc. Report 26, pp. 17–36; Fornander, Bishop Museum Memoirs 6:74.

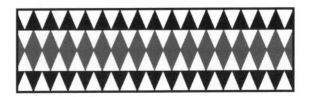

THE BRINDLED DOG

Pa'e was a large, brindled dog that came from somewhere in the Ko'olau Mountains on O'ahu to seek adventure in the villages that border the sea.[1]

All went well until she was spied by the servants of a chief, who thought what a fine feast she would make for the chief if she were cooked in an oven.[2] So they caught and roasted her, and after placing her in a good-sized calabash, they tied a net about the calabash, thrust a pole through the handle of the net, and started on their homeward journey. Ascending a narrow mountain trail, with their load swinging from the pole between them, they reached the top of a cliff and there saw a pretty woman with reddish brown hair sitting beside a pool of water.[3]

She called, "Pa'e ē! Pa'e ē!"

"Here I am!" answered the dog from the calabash.

"Where are you going?"

"I am going with these men to visit the land of the chief."

The men were so frightened that they stood rooted to the spot.

"Come here to me, Pa'e ē! Let us go home together," said the woman.[4]

Pa'e immediately jumped out of the calabash. She showed no trace of the roasting; she was once more the sleek, fat, brindled dog from the mountains.

She ran with delight to her mistress, who, throwing her arms about her, dived with her into the depths of the pool.

The frightened men, realizing that this dog was the pet of one of the lizard women of the Ko'olau Mountains, ran away as quickly as they could, not daring to look behind them.

From that day, brindled dogs were looked upon with superstitious awe in Hawai'i, and considered to be under the protection of the spirits of the lizard goddess, and a brindled dog is called 'īlio mo'o or "lizard dog" to this day.

44

1. *Brindled* refers to the color and marking of the dog's coat—gray or golden brown, spotted or streaked with a darker hue. [Ed.]

2. Dog meat, generally of a special breed of dogs fattened for the purpose, furnished the main roast dish at a Hawaiian banquet. It was roasted for several hours in an underground oven between hot stones so as to preserve all the juices. The *kekeko*, or small dog—sometimes called "*poi* dog" because fattened on *poi*—was in ancient times allowed as food for the women of the household. Men ate pork, which was taboo for women.

3. Pure Hawaiians with a trace of reddish coloring in the hair, which makes it brown, are not uncommon in certain parts of the islands and are called *'ehu,* "dusty."

4. The dialogue in Hawaiian runs as follows:

"Pa'e ē! Pa'e ē!"

"Eō!"

"E hele ana au i ka 'aue'āina o lākou nei."

"E ho'i mai, e Pa'e ē, e ho'i mai kāua."

The word *'aue'āina* is archaic and means "to visit the land of a ruling chief."

THE DOG PA'E

Pa'e was a *kupua* who could change herself into a woman, a *mo'o*, or a brindled dog. She was never known to attack anyone without cause.

One day, when she had assumed her dog body and was playing about on the seashore, an old couple saw her and carried her home to fatten and eat, for at that time she looked too thin to make a good meal. But after several weeks of feeding with sweet potato and gravy, her body grew fat and round. Leaving his wife to prepare the underground oven, the old man went to the uplands to gather taro and sweet potatoes. At home, the old lady prepared the oven and then sat resting in the house. Outside, she heard two strange voices. One said, "Aloha, Pa'e! What a beautiful plump woman you have become!"

"There is no beauty in the day of death," replied the other voice.

"Who is designing your death?" inquired the first voice.

"Alas! Those whom I have allowed to become my masters. The old man has gone to the uplands after vegetables while the old woman is preparing the oven to cook me in."

"Then you take one, I will take the other," replied the first voice.

The frightened woman peeped out to see who was speaking and saw a great, brindled dog talking with the little dog that she had tied up.

Just then, her husband came up with his baskets of taro and potato. He called to his wife and was about to kill Pa'e at once when the strange dog sprang upon him and killed him. Pa'e chewed herself free from the rope that tied her, sought the old woman in the house, and made short work of her.

The two dogs then left the island of Hawai'i and came to O'ahu and made their home in Nu'uanu Valley, where Pa'e is known as "the dog of Ko'olau." The brindled dog who was her rescuer and the woman with reddish brown hair who called her to life in the previous story were one and the same person, a very close friend and companion of Pa'e.

THE 'OAU

Many varieties of 'o'opu, or gobies, are known in Hawaiian waters. *Nāpili* and *nākea*, together with the *'oau*, about which this story tells, are the common kinds. *Nāpili* are used at the ceremony called *māwaewae* to ensure milk to the nursing mother.[1] *Pili* means cling to, as in the expression "Pili ka pōmaika'i, pili ka u'i," may you be prosperous and beautiful—literally, may prosperity and beauty of proportion cling to you.

Some varieties of 'o'opu belong to particular localities. A Kaua'i kind is called *'ōkuhe*. The *pao'o* lives in the sea and is hard to catch because it leaps out of the net.[2] The *nāwao, kauleloa, kāni'o,* and *hi'ukole* live in mountain streams. The *hi'ukole*, or red tail, brings bad luck in the net, since it keeps other fish away. If one is taken, it should be thrown out with an exclamation of disgust in order that the fisherman may have a successful catch.

The *ʻoau*, called *ʻōkuhekuhe* on Oʻahu, lives in either salt or fresh water. Its markings resemble those of the lizard, and it is probably for this reason that the Hawaiians are especially averse to eating this species, owing to the superstitious awe with which they regard the *moʻo* family. The following story tells why for a long time people of Molokaʻi and West Maui would not touch the *ʻoau* found in their waters.

In days long gone by, a certain man living on Molokaʻi went one day to the brook to fish for *ʻoʻopu*. He caught some and returned to the house and kindled a fire, cleaned the fish, and placed them between several layers of *ti* leaf, called *lāʻī*, doubling the leaf over and tying it firmly at one end to keep the fish from falling out.[3]

When the fire had burned down to coals, he placed the bundle of fish upon it and went to mix a calabash of *poi*. While doing so, he heard a voice saying, "Mix it well, and when your vegetable food is ready, you think that I shall serve as meat, I—*ʻoau!*"[4] The man was so frightened that he left his *poi*-mixing and his roasting fish and ran to a friend's house to tell of his amazing experience.

This story was told by Mrs. Annie Aiona and others, and translated by Laura C. S. Green. For beliefs and customs connected with the *ʻoʻopu*, see Fornander, Bishop Museum Memoirs 5:510–514.

1. The ceremony is described by Miss Green in *American Anthropologist* 26:241 (1924).

2. In one variant of the story of Mikololou, the big shark from Hawaiʻi escapes the snare set at the entrance of Pearl Harbor by changing himself into an *ʻoʻopu* and leaping over the snare.

3. The leaves of the *ti* plant *(Cordyline fruticosa)* are used not only for wrapping food but also for thatching, for baskets, and for ceremonial purposes. For Hawaiian cooking, see Kepelino, Bishop Museum Bulletin 95:160–164 (1932). The process here described is called *lāwalu*.

4. A play on words, since the word *ʻoau* is that by which a speaker designates himself, hence, literally, "myself."

THE STORY OF THE ʻOʻOPU

Hawaiians used to believe that the ʻoʻopu,[1] or freshwater goby, belonged to the great moʻo family along with brindled dogs, mermaids or ʻehu women,[2] and especially all lizards.[3] To anyone who had a moʻo as an ʻaumakua, or family guardian spirit, the eating of the ʻoʻopu was taboo.

One day a woman named Kahīnano, Pandanus Blossom, went to the adjacent creek to catch ʻoʻopu for her evening meal. After cleaning and salting the fish, she went to a pandanus grove to gather the long leaves to weave into mats, for the day of the hoʻokupu (the day for paying tribute to the chief of the district) was drawing near.[4]

The sun was just about to set as she started for home. Nearing the house, she spied an ʻehu woman who seemed to be searching for something. Every now and then the woman peered under the brush, beneath the trees, or around the corner of the house. Then, with a sigh, she turned toward the creek. In a loud voice she called, "ʻO Kāniʻo!"[5]

"Here I am," answered the kāniʻo in Kahīnano's house, jumping out of the calabash and running back to the creek.

"ʻO Nākea!" she called, and the nākea quickly responded and returned to the creek.

"ʻO ʻAilehua! ʻO ʻApohā! ʻO Nāpili! ʻO Hinana!" she shouted, and one by one they answered to their names.[6]

As each ʻoʻopu came out of the hut, Kahīnano saw that it seemed to have feet and legs not unlike those of the common house lizard. Terrified, she vowed never to eat any more ʻoʻopu.

This story is often told to prove the relationship of the ʻoʻopu to the moʻo family. If the ʻoʻopu was born into a human family, it was counted as a moʻo even though it was only a simple fish. It was only after the missionaries came and taught the natives that there was no other god but Jehovah that the worshipers of the moʻo gods learned that ʻoʻopu was a good fish to eat. Before that, they feared the anger of the gods would fall upon them and cause their descendants to suffer if they should eat its flesh.

This story was related by Mrs. Wiggin.

1. For beliefs about the *'o'opu* and about Holu, god of the *'o'opu,* see *Fornander Collection* 5:510–514, where the origin of *'o'opu* worship is explained and the methods described for making the sluices and baskets for trapping *'o'opu.*

2. *'Ehu* refers to the reddish tinge seen in the hair of some Polynesians.

3. Compare with the story of the Brindled Dog earlier in the collection. The *mo'o* seems to be regarded as an earthquake deity and to be for this reason connected with the goddess of the volcano. Pools of water formed in earthquake cracks are believed to be inhabited by *mo'o,* and two pools, one at Kalapana in Puna district and the other some miles distant, are supposed to contain the head and the tail of a gigantic *mo'o* whose body stretches beneath the earth between them. The common house lizard is also called *mo'o* and regarded with superstitious awe. See the part played by the friendly *mo'o* who is the guardian of Paliuli in the Lā'ieikawai story, and the *mo'o* who provides for her grandson 'Aukelenuiaiku in Fornander's story of that name. The relationship of the *mo'o* to the Pele family is not too clear, for the conquest of unfriendly *mo'o* is recounted by Emerson in the Pele legend. [M.W.B.]

4. The word used is *pūhala.* *Pūhala* means a grove of pandanus or an old pandanus tree.

5. The *kāni'o* is a striped variety of *'o'opu.*

6. The names represent other varieties of *'o'opu,* all distinguished by specific markings on their bodies.

KAMANU AND THE MO'O

Kamanu was a strong, handsome man who lived with his parents, sisters, and brothers not far from a river where a *mo'o wahine*, or lizard woman, had her cavern.

Daily he went to and from this river to fetch water or to get a few shrimp and freshwater fish for supper. One morning, while engaged in fishing, he felt himself grasped by a pair of arms. He was carried under to a cavern at the bottom of the stream, and there he was released. "Aloha!" said his captor. Kamanu turned to look. He saw a slim woman with reddish brown hair, and terror seized him as he remembered the tales his mother had told him about the *'ehu mo'o* women. He looked about for means of escape but found none. "Don't be afraid," she said. "You will be my husband and I will see to it that your family is supplied with shrimp and fish." Kamanu readily consented, and the woman cared for him well, giving him only the best of food. In the meantime, his parents looked for his body, believing that he was dead. Not finding it, they supposed it had been carried downstream to the beach and there had been devoured by sharks.

After a year, Kamanu grew homesick and ceased to relish his food. "Alas! What grieves my husband?" asked his wife.

"Love for my parents," he replied.

"Then tomorrow I will take you to the surface. Go, visit your parents and come back to the river; there I will wait. Remember to kiss no one until you have kissed your father; if you kiss another first, you will see me no more."

Kamanu went home the next day with a happy heart. Just as he stooped to enter his father's doorway, Makani, his dog, ran out to greet him. Kamanu patted his head. With a howl of delight, Makani leapt up and licked his face.

The family was overjoyed to see Kamanu again. He told them of his wife and their pleasant home at the river bottom. Toward evening, he went back to the river and saw his wife weeping for him. "Goodbye, my husband, you will not see me again," she said and dived into the water.

Day by day, Kamanu went to the bank and called her, but she came no more. He grieved so much that in a few months he died. His father buried him in a cave overlooking the river where he had once lived happily with his bride.

This story was related by Mrs. Wiggin. A modern European, fairy-mistress folktale with a Polynesian coloring, but interesting because it shows how the thing is done. Compare Rice, *Hawaiian Legends*, 91, where a girl cast out by her parents is cared for by a *mo'o*. [M.W.B.]

'IOLE THE RAT AND PUEO THE OWL

'Iole the Rat and Pueo the Owl were *kupua* who lived in Kohala. Pueo was a farmer. Every night he worked, and when the sun rose he rested, for his eyes were blinded by the sunlight. 'Iole, on the other hand, was an indolent, ill-bred fellow who depended on his wit in thievery. He constantly stole sweet potatoes from Pueo, who watched to pounce upon him.

'Iole at last realized that Pueo was carefully watching his steps to the potato patch, so he dug an underground passage which reached the garden and ate potatoes until he was satisfied.

Not seeing 'Iole coming to steal, Pueo concluded that he had gone away and began to be careless. One night, Pueo went to pull potatoes for himself and saw that the greater number of them were gone and many of those remaining had been eaten away except the small portion fastened to the stem.

Great was his wrath, and he sought a way to revenge himself. So he watched for the human keeper, who was filling a gourd with water for

'Iole. When the water gourd was filled, Pueo flew to the gourd and pecked a hole in it. The man seized a stick of wood and struck Pueo, and one of his legs was broken.

Pueo called to 'Io the Hawk, the strongest of the *kupua*, "O 'Io! O 'Io! I have been hurt by the man."

"Who was to blame?" asked 'Io.

"I was," answered Pueo.

"What did you do?"

"I pecked the water gourd of 'Iole."

"Shame on you! You are indeed at fault," said 'Io. "Why did you act so foolishly?"

Pueo wept and said he was hungry because all his potatoes had been stolen. 'Io looked at the keeper and saw that the man's strength was greater than his own; therefore he could not help.

Pueo waited until his leg was well and then sought means of injuring 'Iole. He went among those who were skillful in rat shooting but found no one who could destroy this upstart. Then he heard of a certain rat-shooting wizard on O'ahu named Pīkoi, the son of 'Alalā the Crow; thereupon he went and made friends with him and told him about the thievery of 'Iole. It was Pīkoi's amusement to destroy rats, so they both sailed for Hilo. Pīkoi went to the top of Ka'uiki hill and looked toward Kohala. He saw 'Iole and shot an arrow at him.[1] As 'Iole the Rat lay tranquilly dreaming, never thinking of danger, he was struck by Pīkoi's arrow and instantly killed. The place where he died was named 'Iole and retains that name to this day.

The Hawaiian-language version of this story, *Ka Mo'olelo o 'Iole me Pueo,* appears on page 123. This story was told by Mrs. Ka'ehuokekai McGiffen of Kohala to Mary Kawena Pukui, who dictated it to Miss Green in Hawaiian. This story contains traditional material. The dialogue is found in an old cat's-cradle chant recorded by Mr. Joseph Emerson in *Vassar Publications* 5:13; and Fornander (in *Fornander Collection* 4:450–463) tells the legend of the famous rat shooter Pīkoiaka'alalā, "Pikoi, Son of the Crow." The incident is in the story of Keaunini in Westervelt's *Gods and Ghosts,* page 181. Mr. Emerson calls the bird the 'Elepaio, "woodpecker." Here the animals are represented as *kupua,* beings who can take either animal or human form at will, but they are treated as in animal form and also as gods, since ʻIole has a human keeper to wait upon his needs. The story is of special interest as the only example I know in Hawaiʻi which approaches the form of the animal trickster story so popular among American Indians and Africans. [M.W.B.]

1. At Kalapana, in Puna district on Hawaiʻi, my old Hawaiian host affirmed, eyes twinkling with fun, that the sorcerer of local tradition, Kālaikini, could "stand at Kalapana and shoot a rat at ʻĀpua," which was a point of land stretching like a faint blue haze into the sea far to the westward. [M.W.B.]

THE EEL AND THE SEA CUCUMBER

Puhi and Lohi were *kupua* who traveled from a foreign land to live in Kona. During the day, one was an eel and the other a sea cucumber, but at night both became handsome men. One moonlight night, two girls went to the beach to bathe in the sea and to catch fish. While they were thus engaged, they were seen by Puhi and Lohi. The two drew near the place where the girls were sitting. The girls were startled to see the two handsome men beside them. Seeing the beauty of the sisters, the men addressed them in soft, persuasive words. The girls quickly responded. When they went home, they said nothing about the two strangers because their father had vowed that they should not have foreigners, who might turn out to be *kupua*, for husbands.

Some months later, the father became suspicious of his daughters' loss of appetite and their eagerness to go to the beach as soon as the sun went down, although they brought nothing home with them. So one night, he followed them without their knowledge. He saw them go to the entrance of a little cave where they sat down, and in order to see what they did, he crept after them and hid behind a small heap of stones beside a tide pool.

He had not waited long, when an eel and a sea cucumber came up out of the pool and turned into men. They did not see him. He watched closely all that went on between them and his daughters; then he saw them go back to the pool and change, one into an eel and the other into a sea cucumber, and disappear into the sea. He hastened home and entered the house before the sisters returned. To their surprise, they were not scolded as usual for returning from the beach without any catch.

One night, after the girls had gone down to the beach, he followed quietly to the shore, and when he saw the two men engaged in making love to his two daughters, he laid his net at the place where he had seen them turn into men. When Puhi and Lohi returned to the pool, they were caught fast in the net. He drew them ashore and pounded them to death with stones. That night he carried them home and baked them.

In the morning, when the sisters arose, the father said, "Did you catch any fish last night?"

"No fish, it was too rough," answered the girls.

"Yes, that is true. I went fishing myself last night and caught only an eel and a sea cucumber. I have cooked them, so come and eat."

"Are you not going to eat with us?"

"No, I have already eaten."

They sat down and ate heartily, then their father said, "Look here! You have eaten the fish forms of your two husbands."

The girls ran outside, and while the father stood by with a big club, they threw up—one a tiny sea cucumber, the other a tiny eel, which tried to get back to the beach. The father killed them both with the club and threw them into the fire and burned them to ashes. The ashes he buried in a waterless land so that they could never come to life. As for the girls, they stayed at home until they found husbands of whom their father approved.

The Hawaiian-language version of this story, *'O Puhi me Loli,* appears on page 127. The influence of *kupua* is limited to a particular locality. A similar story is told of an eel *kupua* at Wai'anae on O'ahu. There, the giant shape of an eel *kupua* can be seen against a cliff, where it was flung by the indignant relative who slew the lover.

ʻIlima Kūkahakai

PEKEKUE

Mānoanoa lived on Molokaʻi. From early childhood, she had a special fondness for squid and was famous for her appetite for them. Every day when the fishing canoes came in, she went down to the shore looking for squid. What she demanded, she worked for, and her reward was a squid. The fishermen did not capture many, but if she found a single tentacle, she was satisfied.

One day, she received a large squid and took it home, hung some of the tentacles on a tree to dry, and cut up the rest, intending to eat it after she had finished her work. She went around the side of the house and was busy over some small piece of work.

She lingered over her work and was startled to hear a voice saying, "Pekekue." Hearing the voice call a second time, "O Pekekue!" she looked up to the roof of her house and saw the squid crawling toward her. The tentacles had fastened themselves again to the head. Mānoanoa stared in terror.

When it came close to her, the squid said, "O Pekekue, eat the tentacles but spare the head!" Then the squid gave a leap and dropped into the spring of water close to where she was sitting and disappeared.

From that day, Mānoanoa was afraid of squid. Never again did she go to the beach to wait for the canoes bringing them in. When her grandchild was born, she called the child "Pekekue," the name by which the squid had addressed her.

The Hawaiian-language version of this story, *Pekekue,* appears on page 129. This story was told by a descendant of the squid eater named Kawahinenohoikaʻāinahui.

57

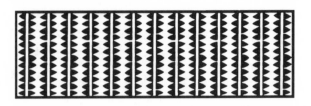

THE MAN WHO WANTED TO EAT SQUID

Because of his fondness for squid, his real name was forgotten and he was called Punihe'e, Squid-lover.

Early in the morning, he was to be seen with his fish-spear and bag woven of pandanus, searching for his favorite food. He knew where the small squid hid clinging to the rocks underwater at the foot of a cliff and where the big longhead had his home.[1]

One morning when he returned with an extra big longhead, a neighbor came to see him. "O Squid-lover," said the neighbor, "perhaps the gods of the ocean will be angry because you catch squid alone; trouble may come to you."

"Nonsense! Do not talk to me of the gods; Punihe'e has no god to help him when he is fishing for squid," replied the fisherman.[2]

This silenced his friend.

Punihe'e soon had a portion of the squid cut up and salted, another portion broiling over a charcoal fire, and a third hung before the door to dry. Both men departed, each to his own vegetable patch.

Just before sundown, the squid-fisher felt the pangs of hunger. He laid aside his digging tool and returned to his hut. There he brought out his calabash of *poi* and the covered dish of salted squid.[3] Then his eyes opened wide with horror: upon uncovering the dish, he saw each piece of the squid roll squirming toward the other, the ends joining and becoming whole tentacles. Punihe'e glanced at the other dish, where he had left the cooked squid; it was acting in a similar manner.

The squid-fisher waited to see no more. Away he ran to tell his nearest neighbor of the antics of the squid. His neighbor could scarcely believe the tale; to prove it, they went together to the squid-fisher's home.

A short distance from the hut, they stopped. The piece of squid drying before the door seemed to be agitated; the pieces that had been put away in the house, both the cooked and the salted, appeared and joined the half-dried piece at the door. In a moment, the squid was whole again. Three of its tentacles were brown, three white, and the rest a very light brown. It climbed up on the hut, and with its tentacles hanging down over the doorway, nodded its head toward the terrified fisherman.

The squid-fisher could bear no more. He fled to the home of the friend who had warned him that morning, and never again was he seen with his fish-spear; when he went to the beach, he carried a fish-pole or net.

And to this day in Hawai'i, a dried squid will squirm when it is placed over hot coals.

1. The little squid is the *he'e pali*. The large one, *he'e pū loa*, lives near the shore, where it is said to climb the pandanus trees in order to watch the shiny-backed lizards, *mo'o 'alā*, which frequent the beach. The favorite squid for food is the *he'e māuli*, or common squid.

2. The word used here for gods is *'aumākua*, denoting a class of ancient family gods still considered able and trustworthy as protectors of certain Hawaiian families, especially of fishermen. The idea here is perhaps that since Punihe'e was employing no supernatural help, there was no fear of his arousing a rival antagonist among the gods.

3. *Poi*, a paste made of the cooked root of the cultivated taro plant, is the chief vegetable food of the Hawaiians—the national dish.

THE WOMAN WHO MARRIED A CATERPILLAR

A good many stories have grown up in the district of Kaʻū which emphasize the awe felt for the little caterpillars, called in Hawaiian ʻenuhe or peʻelua. It was in this way that the worship of peʻelua, armyworms, began in Hawaiʻi.

Kumuhea, son of the god Kū, fell in love with a certain young woman and took her as his wife. No one knew that he could change himself into a huge caterpillar; they only thought of him as a handsome young man.

After his marriage, Kumuhea spent his nights as a worm, eating sweet potato leaves, and returned home in the morning. Being soft and flabby like a worm, he did not know how to work to support his wife and expected her to pick up whatever she could for food.

As she grew thinner and thinner through starvation, she reported her distress to her father, and he inquired where her husband went at night. In order to track her husband, she tied a hemp string to him (attached to the appendage found on the back of a caterpillar), which uncoiled as he went out.

But the string tangled on a bush and Kumuhea discovered the trick. This made him so angry that he returned home to attack all the potato patches in the vicinity, after first taking his unfortunate wife to Puʻuʻenuhe, Hill of the Caterpillar, the hill in Kaʻū where he made his home.

So destructive did Kumuhea become that the people appealed to Kāne to save them. Kāne discovered the god near the hill-cave and cut him up into tiny bits, in which size the caterpillar remains to this day.

So the Hawaiians feel that the leaves of their potato patches belong to the old god Kumuhea, who appears today in the form of a little worm.

THE MAN WHO KILLED CATERPILLARS

On Hawai'i, between Nā'ālehu and Wai'ōhinu, is a low piece of land, sloping toward Wai'ōhinu, that is called Wahamo'o, Lizard's Mouth. The following story is told about this locality.

On the land now called Wahamo'o, there lived two men who cultivated sweet potatoes. One was named Kīlauname, the other Maunakeleawe. A pile of rocks divided their patches; Kīlau cultivated on the Nā'ālehu side and his companion on that toward Wai'ōhinu.

When they planted their gardens, caterpillars swarmed over the vines. Kīlau's companion gathered them into baskets made of pandanus leaves, carried them a great distance off, and left them, saying, "Go, caterpillars, go! Eat all you want of the leaves but leave what is in the earth. Kīlau did not follow this procedure; after picking up the caterpillars, he would tear them in two and throw the dead bodies around. The more he tore, the more that came. They ate all the leaves and all the potatoes, too. He got so angry that he made a large earth oven, and gathering basket after basket of caterpillars, he threw them into the fire. But there were so many that their bodies extinguished the fire. Then he made a larger oven and repeated the process. His companion, meanwhile, had quantities of potatoes, although there were no leaves on the vines.

One day, Kīlau went to the beach. His companion heard voices proceeding from Kīlau's potato patch. One voice called, "Where is Kīlau? Can you see him?" Another answered, "No, can you?" Several said, "He killed many of us—now it is our turn." Then they shouted together, "Kīlau! Kīlau! Kīlau!"

When Kīlau returned from the beach, the voice exclaimed, "Here he comes, here he comes—here comes Kīlau!" Kīlau heard them and mocked them by repeating, "Here's Kīlau, here's Kīlau—what about Kīlau?" All the voices then exclaimed, "Hide, brothers, hide!" When Kīlau came to the middle of his patch, he heard one voice cry, "Advance, brothers, and surround him toward the sea, toward the mountain, toward the sunrise and the sunset—on all sides!"

Then his companion was startled to see caterpillars climbing up on Kīlau from all sides, every caterpillar with two heads. Kīlau tried to fight them off, but they were too many. They entered his eyes, nose, and mouth.

His companion dropped his spade and ran to Nā'ālehu to tell the people the news that Kīlau was being eaten up by caterpillars. The people left their homes and followed Kīlau's companion to the potato patch to see this awful thing, and they found Kīlau just the color of a baked sweet potato! Visible in the dust were tracks made by the little caterpillars.

Since then, no sweet potato patches have been planted at Wahamo'o, and no genuine Ka'ū Hawaiian is guilty of killing a caterpillar. If the *kuawehi*, a large gold- and green-striped caterpillar, attacks a potato patch, it is a sign that a member of the household has transgressed by killing a caterpillar, and probably there will be no crop.

Some Hawaiians believe that caterpillars migrate to the sea when they get tired of living upon land and turn into sea cucumbers.

THE SEVENTH DISTRICT

This story tells why certain people in Ka'ū district, on Hawai'i, take great care of their calabash containers made from the bitter gourd plant.

It is said that there was once a chiefess in Ka'ū who was much loved by her people. When she was about to have a child, she fell ill, and just before the child was to be born, she died. Her body was carried to the burial cave. A great stone was rolled over the mouth of the hole.

On the day when the child was to be born, a sprout appeared from the navel of the chiefess and grew out through a small opening at the entrance of the cave and crept away to a considerable distance. One day, the chief of the seventh district saw that a bitter gourd had crept along and was growing well just behind his house. He watched it blossom and bear fruit. As the gourd ripened, he went every day to thump and pinch it to see if it was ripe enough to cut. Little did the chief know that this bitter gourd was a human being.

The spirit of the gourd went to a medium to complain of the harsh treatment which it was suffering. The *kahuna* of that place was brought, and the bitter gourd showed him what was being done to its body and commanded that it be found and brought back. The priest went to the burial cave and followed the vine as far as the seventh district. The chief, seeing him beside the bitter gourd, asked him what brought him there. The priest replied that he had come at the command of his master. When the chief saw what a fine gourd it was, he refused to give it up. The two disputed over the matter until the *kahuna* suggested that they go to see, by following the stem, who had the rightful ownership of that bitter gourd, for the chief would not believe that it was a human being. The chief agreeing, they went to see from what place the gourd sprouted. They followed the stem to the burial cave and went in. They both saw that the gourd grew out of the abdomen of the chiefess.

The *kahuna* brought back the bitter gourd and guarded it as a beloved child until his own death. After that time, it is not known exactly what became of the bitter gourd. To the family of the chiefess who died, the bitter gourds became sacred objects. If one were broken, it was buried with care or burned so that it might not rot. If anyone asked why the pieces were not thrown away, the answer always was, "Because of the seventh district."

The Hawaiian-language version of this story, *Ka Hiku o nā Ahupuaʻa*, appears on page 130. This story was told by Kaʻehuokekai McGiffen.

Kumuhana liked nothing better than to go out at night to catch the *kōlea* and *'akekeke*.[1] With his nets stained with candlenut, he would creep up to the sleeping birds and capture them.[2] Very often he took more than he needed, and greed kept him from sharing them with others. Instead, he gathered the birds into heaps, and what he did not eat, he left to decompose. He was so fond of the flesh that he could not wait for the birds to be thoroughly broiled and ate them as soon as the outside was slightly browned.

His nearest neighbor was a man who worshiped the great spirit who watched over the *kōlea*, Kumukahi by name. This man had often suffered from illness through inhaling the odor of the broiling birds.[3] One evening when returning from fishing, he met Kumuhana on his way to snare birds for the morrow's breakfast. As they were discussing the events of the day, they heard a long-drawn, plaintive "Pi-i-i-o!" coming from the clouds.

"If I were you, Kumuhana," said the neighbor, "I would go home. I think the spirit of the bird-god goes forth this night to see that all is well with his feathered and human children."

"That is for you to heed," answered Kumuhana, "for no *kōlea* was ever born into my family; therefore, I do not care for them except for eating!" Then, throwing his net over his shoulder, he went forward on his errand of destruction.

Birds by the hundred nestled on the rocks that night. Kumuhana caught enough to last a long time and laid them in heaps as he passed from one rock to another. As dawn broke, he returned. His birds had disappeared during the night!

Suspicious of his good neighbor, he marched straightaway to that person's house and accused him of the theft. "Alas! I know nothing of your birds," was the answer.

"If I were sure you were the thief, I would kill you!" said Kumuhana.

"Hark! Your birds are calling from your own house," exclaimed his neighbor.

Sure enough, from Kumuhana's own house came the whistling and calling of innumerable birds. Kumuhana said no more and hurried

64

Kukui

home. Upon opening the door, he saw his house filled with black pebbles[4] but not a bird was to be seen. Enraged, he went back to his neighbor. "How dare you fill my house with rocks?" he shouted.

"I know nothing of rocks," was the answer. "If I were you, I would ask the pardon of Kumukahi; it may be that he is the one who put the pebbles there. Hark! There are the birds at your house now!"

Sounds of birds issued from the door. Hurrying home, Kumuhana looked inside. Hundreds of birds were within. Quickly, he prepared his earth oven and made the stones red-hot. Then he entered the house and reached for the bird nearest him; it passed through his fingers like vapor. Each time he clutched it, it went through his hands.

Then Kumuhana heard outside the cry "Pi-i-i-o!" With one accord, the birds arose and pecked and scratched the poor man. He ran out-of-doors; more birds awaited him there. Pained and blinded, he stumbled into the pit of the oven he himself had prepared, and there he perished.

To this day, the spot where his house stood is called ʻAiākōlea, that is, "Impiety to the plover." It lies between Waikapuna and ʻAkihinui in Kaʻū district.

The Hawaiians say that when the plover call "pi-o!" over any dwelling, it is an omen of death.

This story was told by Mrs. Wiggin.

1. The Pacific golden plover and the ruddy turnstone are migrants to Hawaiʻi from Alaska, where they breed, appearing in Hawaiʻi about the middle of August to November and leaving in April or May. [M.W.B.]

2. The juice of the *kukui* or candlenut makes a dark stain.

3. According to Hawaiian folk belief, if smoke blows upon a man from a neighbor's oven where an animal sacred to that man is cooking, he has committed an offense against his god and will be punished with illness unless he expiates the offense by offering and prayer. [M.W.B.]

4. *ʻAlā* in the Hawaiian tongue.

THE STORY OF PĀʻAO AND LONOPELE

Two brothers, Pāʻao and Lonopele, were priests of the gods Kū and Lono in ʻUpolu, Sāmoa.[1] Pāʻao was the priest of Kūkāʻilimoku, Kū the Snatcher of Islands, who later became the war god of Kamehameha I.[2]

Pāʻao and Lonopele each had a son, whose pranks often led to quarrels between the fathers. One day, Lonopele's son entered the temple and stole a bit of the food placed for the sacrifice. Lonopele accused the son of Pāʻao. A few days later, Lonopele's son stole more of the sacrifice, and his father seized the son of Pāʻao and had him put to death. Pāʻao was deeply grieved, and in his heart he knew that Lonopele's son was at fault. He watched closely and was rewarded by seeing him run out of the temple with a bit of the offering in his hand. Then Pāʻao put Lonopele's son to death and hid his body under the canoes.[3] For days, Lonopele looked for his son, and when at last he found him, he ordered his younger brother Pāʻao to depart and seek a new home.

Pāʻao went to Tahiti, where he gathered a number of followers who called themselves the *manahuna,* sometimes called *manahunanukumū* or bug-mouthed *manahuna,* because of the daintiness of their mouths. These sailed for Hawaiʻi with Pāʻao.[4]

On the way, a lizard *kupua* begged to join them and was allowed to do so. *Kupua* after *kupua* from the different islands joined the company. One was Makapuʻu, after whom Makapuʻu Point on Oʻahu was named; another was her sister ʻIhiʻihilauākea, for whom a hill near Koko Head was named;[5] and the little, hunchbacked Mālei is still to be seen in the shape of a stone near the lighthouse at Makapuʻu.

This stone goddess was removed into the city of Honolulu for a while until all her caretakers died, at which time she was returned to the shore. She had the power to take the form of either a woman or of a stone, identified from other stone *kupua* by the feather cloak which is carved on her back. With the exception of the lizard *kupua*, all these wizards who left their homes to go to Hawaiʻi were female *kupua*.

While Pāʻao and his friends were crossing the ocean, Lonopele resorted to sorcery and called upon his gods to destroy his brother. Pāʻao and his company prayed to Kanakaokai, Man of the Sea, who was its ruler, to save them. Kanakaokai sent millions of *ʻōpelu*, mackerel, to swim around the canoe of Pāʻao and lift it above the waves. When the storm abated, they disappeared. Again the storm arose, sent by Lonopele. A second time Pāʻao beseeched the god of the sea for protection, and this time another fish, *aku*, the skipjack tuna, came to the rescue and carried the company to land in safety.[6]

They landed at Puna on the island of Hawaiʻi. There Pāʻao built the temple of ʻAhaʻula, or Red Assembly, so named because of the red feather cloaks worn by the god Kūkāʻilimoku and the other gods.[7] He left priests there to care for the temple and to cover the lava rock with soil brought in pandanus baskets from the hill country, to plant rare trees, and dig a well, thus making an oasis in that desert place.[8]

The priests kindled a fire in the temple grounds, which was consecrated to their gods and kept burning night and day. Whatever man the smoke of that fire fell upon, whether high or low in rank, became a sacrifice to the gods. Hence the name of that temple was changed to Wahaʻula, Red Mouth, because it devoured men.[9]

Pāʻao went to Pākaʻālana in the Hāmākua district of Hawaiʻi, where he built another temple. There he left two white stones which were worshiped by the inhabitants of that district,[10] especially by the high chief, Līloa.[11]

Pāʻao saw how the chiefs had sinned by intermarriage with commoners, thus diluting the sacred blood. He sailed back to Tahiti and returned with a chief and his family from there to restore the ancient rank of chiefs in Hawaiʻi. This chief was Piliʻaoʻao, ancestor of Kamehameha I.[12] Pāʻao set him up as the highest ruler on Hawaiʻi and served Piliʻaoʻao until his death. The son of Pāʻao served the son of Piliʻaoʻao and so on for succeeding generations. Hewahewa, who was high priest in the time of Kamehameha I, was a descendant of Pāʻao, and in 1819, when King Liholiho broke the taboo, Hewahewa was the first man to apply the torch to his temple and reduce his ancestral gods to ashes.

An ancient prayer composed by Hewahewa, after he had heard of Christianity through the few white men living at the islands, was printed many years ago both in Hawaiian and in English by a man named Peter Pascal in *Kū'oko'a*, a newspaper published weekly in Honolulu.[13]

HEWAHEWA'S PRAYER

Arise, stand up, stand
Fill up the ranks, stand in rows, stand,
Lest we be in darkness, in black night,
　　　Ye thorny-hearted, assemble a multitude, stand.
　　　A great God, a mighty God,
　　　A living God, an everlasting God,
Is Jehovah, a visitor from the skies;
　　　A God dwelling afar off in the heights
　　　　　At the farther end of the wind,
　　In the rolling cloud floating in the air.
A light cloud resting on the earth,
　　　A rainbow standing on the ocean
　　　　Is Jesus, our Redeemer.
By the path from Kahiki to us in Hawai'i he comes,
From the zenith to the horizon,
　　　A mighty rain from the heavens.
　　　　Jehovah, the Supreme, we welcome,
Sing praises to the rolling heavens,
　　　Now the earth rejoices,
　　　We have received the words
Of knowledge, of power, of life.
　　　Gather with the crowded assembly
　　　　　In the presence of the ever mighty Lord,
　　　　　　Pray with reverence to Jehovah
For a mighty priest of the islands,
　　　Who like a torch will reveal our great sins
　　　　That we may live,
　　　　　　Live through Jesus. AMEN.

This story was told by Mrs. Kanui Kaikaina of Hilo, Hawai'i, and dictated to Miss Green by Mary Kawena Pukui.

1. Other versions of the Pā'ao tradition have been published:

Thrum, *More Hawaiian Folktales,* Chicago, 1923, pages 46–52.

Westervelt, *Hawaiian Historical Legends,* New York, 1923, pages 65–78.

Fornander, *The Polynesian Race,* London, 1878–1880, vol. 2, pages 33–38.

N. B. Emerson, "Long Voyages of the Ancient Hawaiians," a paper read before the Hawaiian Historical Society, May 18, 1893, and published as no. 5 of the papers of the Society, pages 5–13.

Malo, *Hawaiian Antiquities,* translated by Dr. Emerson (1835–1836), Honolulu, 1898, page 25.

Emerson and Thrum follow the same source, that of S. M. Kamakau, an old Hawaiian authority. Westervelt does not cite his authority. Malo is said to differ from Kamakau in placing the home of Pā'ao in the Tongan rather than the Samoan group. The Pā'ao company is supposed to belong to the second period of migration to Hawai'i and their arrival to date from the eleventh century, but the story cannot be vouched for as historically reliable. [M.W.B.]

2. Alexander (*Brief History of the Hawaiian People,* page 41) describes this god as "of wicker-work, covered with red feathers, with eyes made of mother-of-pearl, and wide gaping mouth armed with sharks' teeth." Other principal gods set up in Hawaiian temples were carved from 'ōhi'a wood. [M.W.B.]

3. Kamakau's account is more dramatic; he makes the father demand that the child's body be cut open to prove his innocence. This is more natural than Westervelt's, which makes the lad himself appeal for exoneration. The story is to be compared with episodes recorded by Grey (*Polynesian Mythology and Maori Legends,* London, 1885) in which family quarrels lead to or accompany the migration of Māori chiefs to New Zealand. Grey's allusion (page 84) to the act of Rata at the sailing of the canoe named Tainui (Great Sea), when he "slew the son of Manaia, and hid his body in the chips and shavings of the canoe," is generally identified with the Hawaiian story, and see also the story of Turi's migration, page 126. [M.W.B.]

4. The association of the Manahuna (Menehune?) people with the migration of Pā'ao does not appear in any other published legend so far as I am aware. The Menehune are little people supposed to represent the original inhabitants of the island. They are so associated with magic that today their place in Hawaiian legend is much like that of the sprites or brownies in folktales. In Rice's legend, they are called "natives of Hawaii" (*Hawaiian Legends,* 33–46), and Thrum has the same tradition (*Hawaiian Folktales,* 107–117). But the relater of this story says that the Manahunanukumū are a different class of people from the Menehune. [M.W.B.]

5. The migration of Pā'ao belongs to the same period as that of Mo'ikeha and 'Olopana, and it is clear from a reference to the story of the migration of Mo'ikeha to Hawai'i, published in the *Fornander Collection,* 4:114, that the two stories draw from the same source. These two *kupua* women are there claimed as the sisters of Mo'ikeha, and the

priest of Moʻikeha has the same name (Moʻokini) as the temple claimed to be erected by Pāʻao in Kohala. Evidently, the two traditions are variants, and both bear so close a resemblance in their introductory episode to Māori migration legends that it seems safe to conclude a common source with Māori tradition. [M.W.B.]

6. Malo makes the two shoals accompany the chief Pili, who later in this story is said to be fetched from Tahiti by Pāʻao, and says, "When the wind kicked up a sea, the *aku* would frisk and the *opelu* would assemble together, as a result of which the ocean would entirely calm down." The old Hawaiians, according to Malo and Alexander, observed a regularly alternating taboo upon *aku* and *ʻōpelu* fishing, the *aku* being free during the winter months and the *ʻōpelu* during the summer. The conclusion of the great winter festival of Makahiki was marked by the ceremonial breaking of the *ʻōpelu* taboo by a representative of the gods, who ate an eye of the *ʻōpelu* fish or of a man sacrificed in place of the fish if the night catch had been unlucky. See Malo, 199, 275. Mrs. Pukui seems to infer that the restricted season was somewhat arbitrarily within the will of the priests. She says, "The *ʻōpelu* and *aku* were considered sacred fish. There was a restricted season (probably known to the priests) when no one dared touch them under penalty of death. When the priests wished an open season, one of them would go out in a canoe and catch one *aku* and one *ʻōpelu* and lay them before their gods. The high priest ate an eye of each. If the priest failed to catch one of these fish, a hook was inserted into the mouth of a human victim, who thus became either *aku* or *ʻōpelu* and was dragged to the temple for sacrifice. A crier announced both the restricted and the open season." [M.W.B.]

7. In *Place Names of Hawaii* (University of Hawaii Press, 1974), Mrs. Pukui and her colleagues give another translation for *ʻAhaʻula*—sacred assembly—using an alternate meaning of *ʻula*. These two meanings are related, since red is the color of royalty. [Ed.]

8. No other account I have of the landing of Pāʻao gives this story of the naming of the famous *heiau*, which is still to be seen on the south coast of Puna and is said to be the best preserved on the island. When I saw it on May 16, 1914, the walls were still partially in place about the rectangular space set off for the *heiau*. The rock of sacrifice was shown in place in the lefthand corner of the end away from the sea, and at the end toward the sea a kind of trench was walled in where the bodies used to be exposed for three days before the bones were cleaned, washed, and taken away for burial. A small, stone platform in the center still showed the postholes where the priests' house had once been erected. Below the *heiau*, on the way to the sea, we passed over rough lava where the gravel had been scooped away at intervals and the soil utilized for growing sweet potatoes. Old Pāʻao, who is said to have planted in this spot specimens of every tree that grew in the islands of the group, would I think have been pleased with this perpetuation of his own interest in agriculture. [M.W.B.]

9. Women were never sacrificed because they were considered polluted. They were killed if they broke a taboo or, if of high rank, had an eye gouged out. The high chief Alapaʻi threw taboo violators of either sex into the sea as "shark bait," *kūpalumanō*.

10. When Abraham Fornander visited the old *heiau* of Moʻokini in 1869, he found at the bottom of a secret well east of the entrance (which had been filled in with stones and

rubbish) two smooth, round stones shaped like those used for the game of *maika* or quoits-pitching (as described by Malo, chapter 45) but very much larger than those actually used for the purpose, "said to be the particular *ulu* which Paao brought with him from foreign lands" and called *Nā ʻulu a Pāʻao*. Fornander described them as follows: "These stones were as large as the crown of a common-sized hat, two inches thick at the edges and a little thicker in the middle . . . of a white, firm-grained, hard stone." See *Polynesian Race* 2:36–38. [M.W.B.]

11. The father of ʻUmi.

12. According to Fornander, the chiefship was first offered to Lonokaʻeho, who refused it and proposed Pilikaʻaiʻea. That most popular of all ancient Hawaiian chants is said to have been uttered by Makuakaumana, the singing priest of the expedition of Pāʻao, upon the occasion of this invitation, as given by Fornander in the *Fornander Collection* 4:201.

Eia nā waʻa kau mai	Here are the canoes, get aboard
E hoʻi e noho iā Hawaiʻi	Come along and dwell in Hawaiʻi
* kuauli*	(with-the)-green-back,
He ʻāina loaʻa i ka moana	A land that was found in the ocean
I hōʻea mai loko o ka ʻale	That was thrown up from the sea,
I ka halehale poʻi pū a Kanaloa	From the very depths of Kanaloa
He koʻakea i hālelo i ka wai	The white coral in the watery cave
I lau i ka makau a ka lawaiʻa	That was caught on the hook of the fisherman,
A ka lawaiʻa nui ʻo Kapaʻahu.	The great fisherman of Kapaʻahu. [M.W.B.]

13. Printed by Mr. Joseph Emerson in his paper "Selections from a Kahuna's Book of Prayers," read before the Hawaiian Historical Society in 1917 and published in its 26th annual report, Honolulu, 1918, pages 36–39. [M.W.B.]

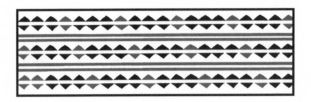

THE DESPOTIC CHIEFS OF KAʻŪ

That district lying between Kona and Puna, Kaʻū, in the old days was called a land of oppression because of three despotic chiefs who lived there.[1] These are tales told about them.

HALAʻEA

A greedy chief was Halaʻea. Every day he visited the fleet of fishing canoes and took for himself and his retainers all the fish he could find. Then he held a feast, carousing and often wantonly wasting the food that remained. As for the fishermen, they were obliged to catch the fish without ever having any to take home to their families. Day after day, they ate herbs for food.

This conduct of the chief greatly vexed the people, and they sought means to rid themselves of his oppression. Never did they go out upon the ocean without hearing on their return the voice of their chief crying, "The fish is mine! Give me the fish!"

At last came the season for ʻahi, the tuna, and a proclamation was made, summoning the head fishermen to accompany their chief to the fishing grounds. So they gathered together and prepared their canoes, looking after the nets, the bait, and whatever else was required for the expedition. Also, they held a council at which it was agreed to deposit all their fish in the chief's canoe and themselves return to the shore without even a backward glance. At the day appointed, everything was in readiness from Waiʻahukini to Keauhou.

When the first canoe-load was conveyed to the chief's canoe, even then the voice of the chief could be heard protesting, "Bring me the fish! Bring me the fish!" But when the second, third, fourth, fifth, and succeeding canoes had deposited their loads into the chief's canoe and he saw there was danger of swamping the canoe with their weight, he called out, "The chief has fish enough!"

"Not so!" cried the men. "Here is all the fish that the chief desires!" They piled in the last load, and the canoe began to sink rapidly. The chief looked about for help, but there was no canoe at hand and no man to show compassion; all had gone back to land.

So perished Halaʻea in the sea, surrounded by the objects of his greed.

KOIHALA

An irresolute chief was Koihala. When the chief was visiting in Kona, he dispatched a messenger to Kaʻū with the order for food to be prepared and taken to Waiʻahukini to meet him. When all was ready, the servants bore it to Waiʻahukini.[2] As they sat awaiting his appearance, they saw the chief's canoe heading for Kāʻilikiʻi, so they took up the food again and went on to the place where they expected him to land. But when they got to Kāʻilikiʻi, he was heading for Kapuʻa.

Again the men shouldered the food and followed toward the mountain, but as they reached Kapuʻa, they perceived the chief heading for Kaʻaluʻalu, and they immediately proceeded thither.

By this time they were hungry and tired, and they therefore agreed to watch and, if the chief did not arrive shortly, to eat the food themselves. The chief delayed landing, simply sitting idly in the canoe and gazing at the men. So the servants ate the food that had been prepared and then they put stones in the *ti*-leaf packets in which the fish had been wrapped[3] and in the empty calabashes of vegetable food. The chief, seeing these things, paddled furiously until he reached Kaʻaluʻalu. Hence has arisen the proverb "Kau ʻino ʻau waʻa o Kaʻaluʻalu," that is, "The canoes arrive hurriedly at Kaʻaluʻalu."

Hastening up the beach to the spot where the men sat, he cried, "Say! Let us eat! Let the chief eat!"

"Yes, indeed!" answered the servants. "Here is vegetable food and fish!" Whereupon they stoned the despotic chief to death.[4]

KOHĀIKALANI

An evil man was the chief, laying heavy burdens upon his people whenever opportunity offered. When he built a temple for himself on the hill Kaʻulakalani,[5] he commanded the men of the place to bring large, smooth stones from Kāwā, many miles distant. Patiently, the heavy loads slung on poles over their shoulders, they bore the rock from the seashore to the hill where the foundation of the temple was to be laid. When much stone had been collected, two priests *(kahuna)* arrived to supervise the erection of the structure, and upon seeing the quantity of stone brought from Kāwā, they turned to the men and exclaimed, "Look you! There was stone enough already without your exerting yourselves to bring more from Kāwā! It is clear that your chief intends when this temple is completed to offer your bodies as sacrifice. Hence, when he commands you to bring an 'ōhi'a tree to be used in the building, you must tell him to select one for himself and that you will then help him pull it up here. In this way you may save your lives."[6]

The people heeded the priests' warning, and when they were commanded to descend the cliff after a tree, they replied, "O heavenly one, listen! It is better for you to choose the tree to your liking and uproot it, and we will haul it up hither." The chief consented. He was so strong that with one pull he uprooted a great tree. He lopped the branches and then proposed to ascend the cliff and pull the tree up from the top while the men pushed from below. This, however, they refused to do; they wanted to pull while the chief pushed from below, and to this the chief acquiesced. The men pulled at the tree until it was half the distance up the cliff, then released the rope. The great tree rolled over on top of the chief, and death came to the oppressor.

Since the rule of these despotic chiefs, Ka'ū has become noted as a land where people look out for themselves and their own family. The rulers fear to say "We are great chiefs" lest a reckoning come from the people. In the old days, Ka'ū was a despotic district; a chief would command and be instantly obeyed—one would give orders which were at once fulfilled. Thus did they live. But these days of civilization have overturned all those customs.

The Hawaiian-language version of this story, *Nā Ali'i ho'oluhi o Ka'ū*, appears on page 131. This story was given by Mrs. Keli'ihue Alakaihu of Ka'ū and written down in Hawaiian by Mary Kawena Pukui. The story of Koihala was told by Miss Katherine Pope in *Hawaii, The Rainbow Land*, 124.

1. See Malo, chapter 18, for the relations existing between the chiefs *(ali'i)* and the common people in ancient Hawai'i. [M.W.B.]

2. Burdens were generally carried on a pole balanced on the shoulders. Articles to be carried were distributed evenly into two packets and hung on the ends of the pole so as to preserve the balance. Food and clothing were packed into large calabashes (of gourds or

hollowed wood), and these were slung in a net *(kōkō)* at each end of the pole.

3. Raw meat was wrapped in *ti* leaves and tied into a neat packet before baking.

4. Compare the similar plot by which the disaffected old followers of Līloa destroyed Hākau and obtained the chieftainship of Hawai'i for 'Umi. See *Fornander Collection* 4:200–204. [m.w.b.]

5. This hill lies back of Hīlea plantation, where the story is still current.

6. Human sacrifices were required for the dedication of a newly built temple and were usually furnished from prisoners of war or from those who had in some way incurred the enmity of priest or chief. For the use in temple building of the *'ōhi'a* tree, one of the loftiest hardwoods of Hawai'i, see Malo, chapter 37.

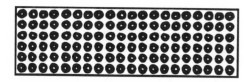

THE STORY OF NĀNAELE

Nānaele was a high chiefess of Ka'alāiki[1] in Ka'ū district on the island of Hawai'i. She was kindly, fair to look upon, and a general favorite with her people.

One day, a company of travelers from Kohala district visited Ka'ū and, seeing Nānaele, coveted her as a wife for their young chief, Nāliko. When this proposition was made to Nānaele, she consented, since they reported him a pleasant man, handsome, modest, industrious, and with other good qualities. On returning to Kohala, the men told Nāliko about the comeliness of Nānaele and begged him to become the husband of so beautiful a woman. Nāliko was delighted that such an excellent wife had been secured for him and readily assented to the arrangement. A few short months later, the two young people were married at Ka'alāiki. Friends and relatives attended the great feast prepared for them. Soon after, Nānaele returned with Nāliko to Kohala.

It was not long before Nāliko returned to his old ways—to the *hula* and the company of young women of the district, leaving Nānaele at home with neither vegetables nor fish. She could do nothing. She could only wait until his affection brought him back to her again, when he would perhaps bring her the food she needed; meanwhile, her body wasted away until she was nothing but bone.

When finally her unfaithful husband returned home, Nānaele turned to him and said, "O Nāliko, listen! A new life for me; I shall never see you. You have provoked me too much with your unkindness!"

"Ugh! If you should live, so should Milu!" responded her husband, and he went off at once to his pleasures.[2]

When her husband was gone, Nānaele crept out in search of food. She crawled along until she came to a place where some farmers raised pigs; there she fell to the ground in her weakness. A man who was passing, seeing that something was causing excitement among the herd of pigs, came to look and found the exhausted woman. He carried her across his shoulders to his hut, where Nānaele was cared for by his wife.

By the time that Nānaele had recovered her strength a little, the rumor had reached Ka'ū district that she was almost dead. This news brought heaviness of heart to the people of Ka'alāiki and Kāwā, and they decided to go and fetch home their chiefess. Some went from Kahuku, some from Kona, still others from Kohala. Two of them went to the place where Nānaele was staying, taking a *mānele*[3] in which she was placed and then borne with care some distance to a place where other men were waiting to relieve the weary bearers of their burden. Thus was she taken by relays until she reached Ka'alāiki.

After a year had passed, Nāliko heard that Nānaele had recovered her health, that she was twice as beautiful as before, and that many suitors from the mountains to the sea were seeking her favor. So this neglectful husband arose and started out to take his wife back to Kohala. Some of the retainers of Nānaele, perceiving his movements, ran to report them to her parents. Nānaele was removed to Kāwā and there concealed. Meanwhile, a great feast was prepared at Ka'alāiki for Nāliko. When he arrived there, he was welcomed by his parents-in-law and informed that his wife and her woman attendants had gone bathing in the sea and would return late that evening.

During the feast, Nāliko was greatly entertained by watching the women dancing and chanting this *mele*, or song:

> For myself, for Nānaele,
> For the wife of Nāliko.
> For me, a new life—
> I shall see you no more.

To which other women answered,

> Ugh! If you should live, so should Milu,
> Who dwells down below!

Nāliko never stopped to consider that this song was meant as a reproach to himself. The men of Kaʻalāiki were planning, when Nāliko was in a tranquil frame of mind and night brought partial darkness over the land, to slay him and hide his body in a secret cave. But an old man was moved to pity in his behalf and whispered secretly to Nāliko, "They mean to kill you! Here! Delay is perilous! I will guide you to a place where you can hide. Come with me!" So when Nāliko saw that the people of the place were not watching, he and the old man fled secretly. They traversed an underground cave, going on and resting, going on and resting, until they reached a spot back of the Kapāpala stock ranch where they ran along between the mountains Hualālai and Maunaloa⁴ until Nāliko could go on alone to his own district while the old man turned back toward Kaʻū lest suspicion fall upon him of having aided the escape. As he went, he saw many men out searching for Nāliko and discreetly joined himself to their number, and they scoured the country from Kahuku to the crater of Pele at Kīlauea.

Nāliko now realized that never again would he possess Nānaele, and love for his patient wife gushed up within him. He recalled how she had said, "You are an unloving husband! A new life for me; I shall never see you again." He knew that he would have been killed without compunction by the men of Kaʻalāiki. As for Nānaele, she was happy to be again with her loving parents and to bring rejoicing to the hearts of her own people.

It is sprinkled; the tale has fled!⁵

The Hawaiian-language version of this story, *Nānaele*, appears on page 134. Related by Mrs. Wiggin after an old Kaʻū tale concerning the doings of certain families of the chiefs of Hawaiʻi.

1. The place-name means small pebbles.

2. The underworld of the dead was said to be ruled over by an ancestor named Milu.

3. A litter shaped like a sedan chair. High chiefs were not allowed to step upon the common earth.

4. These mountains tower 8,269 feet and 13,675 feet above sea level, respectively.

5. An old form of concluding a tale, not much in use today.

THE LAW OF THE SPLINTERED PADDLE

On one occasion when Kamehameha I was building a *heiau* (temple) and needed human sacrifices, sometimes as many as ten persons were made victims, for the greater the number sacrificed, the greater the power conferred upon the temple. [To secure fresh victims], he started along the coast in a canoe with his retainers. At one place, they saw two fishermen walking on the shore. Bidding his retainers to remain at a distance, Kamehameha endeavored to capture the men. When they saw they were being pursued, both fled.

Just as he was about to grasp the nearer man, Kamehameha's foot caught in a fissure of lava, and he fell. The man he was chasing instantly struck him over the head with his paddle, a blow so hard that the paddle was splintered.

"Why don't you kill him?" said his companion.

"Life is sacred to Kāne," replied the man, quoting the old saying "Ua kapu ke ola na Kāne."[1]

Kamehameha had regained consciousness after the blow and heard what the two men were saying. He knew the man could easily have killed him by running a fish-spear through his body and that neither of the two had recognized him as their chief. The chief was so impressed with the two men's reverence for life that he put an end to human sacrifice and promulgated the famous "Law of the Splintered Paddle," which runs: "E hele ka 'elemākule, a me nā luahine, a me nā keiki, a moe i ke ala." "Let the old men, the women and children sleep [in safety] by the wayside."

This story was told by Kaluhiokalani, a relative of Mary Kawena Pukui, who also told the Kamehameha story. *Kānāwai Māmalahoe* (Law of the Splintered Paddle). A more circumstantial version of this story is in Westervelt's *Hawaiian Historical Legends,* 162–175, where a quite different account is given of the event.

1. See *Fornander Collection* 4:266. Fornander thinks that the worshipers of the god Kāne did not demand human sacrifices.

A STORY OF KAMEHAMEHA I

After the battle of Kamehameha against Kalanikūpule, at the time of the leaping of the *'anae*,[1] a certain soldier came before the attendants of the king[2] and boasted, saying that he was Kamehameha's own brother.

When the counselor[3] heard this, he was very angry and said, "Insolence![4] Who told you, you braggart,[5] that you were related to the divine one?[6] This is excessive and vain."[7]

"Yes, it is true," answered the man, "I am his younger brother,[8] and he is the first-born."

When the counselor heard these words, he was filled with wrath. "Only one younger brother has the divine one, namely Keli'imaika'i— not you, impertinent one!"[9]

Here the conversation ended. The counselor went before the king and told him all that he had heard from the man.

Then the king commanded, "Go and fetch this mischievous person,[10] and bring him before me."

When the man came, he crawled on his hands and knees before the king. The king arose and said in a loud voice, "Listen! Is it true, this thing that I have heard, that you, boaster, have called me, the king, your elder brother?"

"Yes, O divine one, it is true."

"And who has told you that you are my younger brother?" asked the king.

"You, O my lord."

"Nonsense! When did I say that to you?"

"When we went to battle on O'ahu of Kākuhihewa,[11] you turned to us and said, 'Forward, my brothers, till you drink the bitter waters!' And hearing these gracious words, O king, has caused me to boast that I am your younger brother. Forward we went together and drank the bitter waters."

When the king heard this just reasoning, he laughed and ordered his retainers to prepare a feast for his youngest brother.

The Hawaiian-language version of this story, entitled *Kekahi Moʻolelo e pili ana no ke Aliʻi Kamehameha* I, appears on page 139.

1. In April 1795, Kamehameha fought a decisive battle against the reigning chief of Oʻahu, Kalanikūpule, and drove the men of Oʻahu over the great Nuʻuanu precipice north of the road. This is the place called "the leaping-place of the mullet," a metaphor drawn from fishing practices.

2. *ʻAialo,* literally, "to eat before," hence those followers of the king who are provided for in his own household. The group is composed of his relatives and intimate friends, who also wait upon, serve, and entertain him.

3. *Pūkaua,* second in command, the king's counselor in peace and companion or leader in war.

4. *Kāhāhā,* an exclamation conveying the emotion of surprise, incredulity, or contempt.

5. *Piʻikoi,* an insulting term used for one who claims honors or rank not due him.

6. *Kalani,* "the heavens, the heavenly one." All chiefs drew their descent from the gods.

7. *Keu* may be translated "over and above" (a certain number) or "it makes me angry," but no word in English quite fits it.

8. *Pōkiʻi,* an endearing appellation used for the younger members of a family.

9. *Keliʻimaikaʻi,* "the good chief," a title earned by the younger brother of Kamehameha because, contrary to custom, he respected the private property of the country people and farmers when, in 1775, he led the expedition for his brother which re-took the districts of Hāna and Kīpahulu from the king of Maui. See Fornander, *Polynesian Race,* 2:229.

10. *Kupu ʻino,* "evil springing."

11. "Kākuhihewa's Oʻahu" because the Kākuhihewa line of chiefs was the most celebrated line of kings of that island in legendary days. Fornander (*Polynesian Race,* 2:272) calls Kākuhihewa "not only one of the great kings of Oahu, but also celebrated throughout the group for all the princely qualities that formed the *beau ideal* of a high-born chief in those days."

TWO STORIES ABOUT KAMEHAMEHA I

I

During his last illness, Kamehameha wished to know definitely on what day he would die. He summoned his priests to appear and asked them, "On what day will the chief die?" The question baffled them and they were silent. The chief ordered a servant whom he trusted to come to him. When the man came, the chief said, "Procure a black pig and go to Maui, to my man Pōpolo. As soon as you reach the island, let loose the pig, and it will guide you to the house. You will have no difficulty recognizing Pōpolo; the pig will fall dead at his feet."

The servant did all that he had been commanded. When he reached Maui, the pig led him on until it fell dead before Pōpolo. Already a revelation had come to Pōpolo that a stranger was coming from Hawai'i bearing bad news concerning the conqueror. He entertained the messenger and, learning from him the chief's wish, agreed to accompany him back to Hawai'i.

As soon as he arrived, the chief asked, "When am I to die?" He answered, "When Hoku comes."[1] The chief then turned to his household and told them what he wished to have done after his death. On the night of Hoku, Pōpolo saw portents in the sky; turning to the people, he cried, "The heavenly one has gone!" On this night Kamehameha I died.

To keep alive the memory of this night, certain chiefs were named Leleiōhoku, Departure to Hoku, because it was on the night of Hoku that the breath of the conqueror left him forever.

II

Before his death, in the days when Kamehameha leaned upon a staff,[1] he gave to Ulumāheihei the name of Hoapili, and from the naming of this man and his wife came the names Hoapilikāne and Hoapiliwahine.[2]

The occasion for the giving of this name to Ulumāheihei was at the

83

calling together of the chiefs to decide which one of them should bury his bones. When they had come together, Kamehameha noticed that the twisted hair ornaments, the whale tooth necklace,[3] and the feather *lei* which had belonged to other chiefs in the past were now being worn by these men. Ulumāheihei was the only chief who wore no such ornament. So Kamehameha said, "You shall not bury me. See! You are boldly disclosing the bones of your chiefs when you wear these things. Only he, Ulumāheihei, my faithful friend, shall be chosen to hide my bones."

The Hawaiian-language version of the first story, *He Moʻolelo e pili ana no Kamehameha* I, appears on page 140. There is no Hawaiian-language version of the second story.

I

Told by policeman Robert Ahuna at an event held on the grounds of the old palace, now the Executive Building in Honolulu; retold in Hawaiian by Mary Kawena Pukui; text and translation by Laura C. S. Green.

Kamehameha I (1736–1819) won control of the island of Hawai'i after the death of his uncle, who was its chief, and brought the entire group of islands under his control. He was the last ruler who kept up the old religious order of the priesthood, the temples, and the *kapu*.

1. Hoku is the fourteenth night after the new moon.

II

This story is told by Joseph L. Kūkahi in his edition of *Ke Kumulipo*.

1. The ages of man are carefully distinguished by Hawaiians, this of the *kanikoʻo* being that when a man is so old as to lean upon a staff *(koʻo)*.

2. Literally, the word means close (or clinging) friend. Hoapili (died 1840) was governor of Maui during the early Christian missions to Hawai'i, and both the husband, Hoapilikāne, and his wife Hoapiliwahine were strong supporters of mission policies.

3. A necklace made of strands of human hair very finely braided, from which hung as a pendant a highly polished hook made from a whale's tooth.

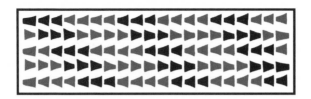

THE STORY OF KEAHIʻĀLOA

Keahiʻāloa, or Eternal Fire, was adopted at birth by her mother's older sister.[1] When she was seven years old, her adopted mother took her from Hawaiʻi, the land of her birth, to live on Kauaʻi.

After their arrival, the mother was drawn into immoral pleasures and soon gave no thought to the child. She was allowed to wander hungry until her body became weak and emaciated and her eyes like the drawn threads of a spider web.

One night, she crawled to the sweet potato patch owned by an aged couple and nibbled those potatoes which she could reach. And because of the long road she had traveled, she soon fell asleep.

When the old woman came the next morning to dig the potatoes and found small bits that had been chewed, she thought the garden must have been invaded by a turtle, and she called to her husband, "Come, old man, let us hunt for this turtle that has been eating our potatoes!" In their search, they found Keahiʻāloa asleep, and great was their joy, for they had no children. They took her home and named her Honu, Turtle.

As the child grew older, it was evident that she possessed gifts of magic and could foretell to her foster parents events yet to happen. She often visited the mountainside and never returned without being adorned in such plants as the sweet-scented *maile,* the scarlet *lehua,* and the royal *mokihana.*[2] Among her favorite pastimes was that of sledding on a grassy slope with the young people of that country.

One day, Keahiʻāloa turned to her foster parents and said, "Listen, grandparents! You have worked hard for me, and now that I see I am a woman, it is right that I should work for you. If you will listen to my counsel, we shall live like chiefs of the land. Tomorrow, let us go to the mountain for taro and ʻawa, and after that to the seashore for every delicacy of the ocean. A stranger is coming who will make me his wife."

Before dawn the next day, they ascended the mountain to pull taro and 'awa root, and they reached home before noon. As day was declining, the taro was cooked and pounded. Near dark they went to the beach, where they very soon had secured all the fish they desired. When all was in readiness, the girl said, "Let us now sleep, and in the early morning my stranger will arrive."

Sure enough, at daybreak a stranger made his appearance, the son of the land agent, who had been inspecting fishponds belonging to the chief and in the darkness had wandered off the path. As it grew light, shivering with cold and half-famished, he had tried to find a familiar place on the path but could not, and instead had reached the house of the old couple.

The old people welcomed the stranger, and their daughter prepared food for him. When the youth's hunger was appeased, he asked the old people, "Say, is this your daughter?"

"Yes, she is ours."

"I should like her to become my wife; what would you think of it?"

"Oh! We are not the ones to marry you; ask her!"

The girl at once assented to his proposal. When noontime came, he went to tell his parents that he had found a wife. They immediately began to prepare a new grass house, mats, barkcloth for bed coverings and clothing, and other things necessary for the young people, planning in ten days to go and fetch her.

About this time, while Keahi'āloa was living on Kaua'i in this manner, a certain man went to the home of her own parents on Hawai'i and told how the mother's sister had neglected the child and how one day she had wandered off and been lost. Hearing all this, the father beat his wife cruelly and scolded her well, saying, "It was not I who gave my daughter away; it was because of your obstinacy that my only garland was given to your older sister. I told you how it would be! You must now make forty fine mats, forty coarse mats, and forty sheets of barkcloth, and if you do not finish them within ten days, I will beat you again so as to hurt you badly!"

Sympathetic relatives collectively labored to achieve this task, and before the time appointed, everything was ready. The parents at once boarded a canoe and started for Kaua'i. During the passage, the father dreamed that his guardian spirit came to him in the form of a shark and said, "Listen! Proceed on your way, and I will be with you. You shall not

'Awa

weary yourself with searching for the child, for I will lead you to her. The house upon which you see a rainbow resting, that is where our garland dwells." So he arose from sleep full of hope that he would again behold his beloved child.

As the day approached for the marriage of the young people, Keahi-'āloa said to the old couple, "Tonight as you sleep, you may be disturbed by rustlings and vibrations, but sleep on until morning." That night they indeed heard sounds, but they lay still until dawn. Upon arising, they saw two large booths covered with coconut leaves built by the side of the house.

The next night, their foster daughter again said to them, "If you hear a noise like the cutting of wood, do not rise." That night the old couple were awakened by a sound like a multitude of men cutting timber, and in the morning they found the space in front of their house filled with carved wooden bowls and platters. Their hearts were filled with amazement at their adopted child's wonderful achievement, and they began to suspect that the companions she had met on the mountain were none other than the little people of the woods, the *menehune,* but they said nothing to her about this.

When night came again, she bade them lie quiet even if they heard the crashing of trees and the sound of chopping. They certainly heard sounds outside, but they did as they were told. In the morning they beheld a huge pile of firewood, but they asked no questions, knowing it was the work of good spirits.

Just as she had instructed them before, so she did when the shadow of the following evening fell. They heard the grinding of stones and smelled smoke, but they were not deaf to the girl's counsel. When the sun rose, the pile of wood was gone, and the bowls were filled with cooked and pounded taro root.

The night following, Keahi'āloa said, "If you hear the sound of the surf and the rattling of pebbles upon the sandy beach, do not rise; sleep until morning, then arise." The surf was high that night, with a sound as if heavy pebbles were being dragged over the shore. In the morning, the old people found all kinds of sea delicacies prepared—shellfish, sea urchins,[3] squid, seaweed, and fish already made savory with salt.

Keahi'āloa gazed over the ocean and said, "Today there will come to our marriage the land agent, his wife, their son, and all their people. And also today will arrive my own parents from Hawai'i. When a rainbow cloud stretches from our house to the ocean, we shall see them landing the canoe. This booth here is prepared for the land agent, that over there for my parents."

When the sun was in mid-heaven, the land agent and his family arrived bearing many gifts. As they were seated, a rainbow cloud like smoke glowed above the ridgepole of the house, and soon after, the parents of the girl stood before them. Then, as the father beheld his one garland, he wept aloud, declaring his love for his child:

> Alas, my garland, my flower!
> You were brought hither to this land of strangers to be
> 	treated cruelly,
> To wander like a homeless cloud!
> O Keahi'āloa, listen!
> O my daughter, you who have faced much suffering!

Now this was the first intimation the old couple had had that Keahi'āloa was the name of their foster child and that she was descended from chiefs. They had never called her anything but "Honu."

The land agent too stood and wondered whether the parents might not forbid the marriage of the young people, but when Keahi'āloa explained how kindly she had been cared for by the old couple and how, out of her great love for them, she had consented to become the daughter-in-law of the land agent, the parents readily consented, and the young people were wedded that very day.

At the close of the feast, Keahi'āloa arose and pronounced this edict concerning her future offspring for all time: that children of a younger brother or sister should not be given in adoption to an older brother or sister, lest they die; only an older brother's or sister's child should be given to a younger, that they might prosper. Hence the descendants of Keahi'āloa have kept this command of their ancestor until this day.[4]

The Hawaiian-language version of this story, *Keahi'āloa*, appears on page 141. A "family story" related in Hawaiian by the grandmother of Mrs. Pukui, Nāli'ipō'aimoku, of her ancestor Keahi'āloa and dictated to Miss Green by Mrs. Pukui.

1. The birth mother is here referred to as *"kona lūau'i makuahine,"* an expression peculiar to the Hawaiian tradition of relationship, according to which a child calls not only its

biological mother but all the women of that generation in the family *"makuahine,"* that is, "mother." [M.W.B.]

2. The plants here listed are sacred to the gods of the forest and are employed for ceremonial purposes, the *maile* for its sweet aroma, the *lehua* for the scarlet blossoms with which it is covered, and the *mokihana* for the strong odor of anise that its pods exude. To pluck these plants without the favor of the gods would undoubtedly bring about sickness or even death. Hence the parents conclude that the girl is under the protection of the little people of the forest, the *menehune*.

3. The *wana* and *hāʻukeʻuke* are two species of sea urchin. The shell of *hāʻukeʻuke* is rounded on the top and flat on the bottom, and its long spikes were used for slate-pencils in the old days.

4. The mother of Mrs. Pukui gave her first-born in adoption to an older sister and the child died; so when Mrs. Pukui was born and the sister asked again for the child, the mother refused and quoted as an excuse the counsel of Keahiʻāloa.

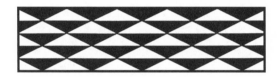

THE ROBBERS OF ʻŌLAʻA

The *ʻōlohe* of ʻŌlaʻa were a band of robbers who lived in caves in the forest.[1] Travelers from Kaʻū to Puna district, from Puna to Hilo, and from Hilo to Kaʻū were attacked, killed, and their bodies hidden away by these robbers.

This is how they did it. One of them would climb a tree and look toward the sea. If he saw no one, the spy called, "Tide is out!" If he saw a few people, he called, "Low tide!" If the group was ten or more, he called, "High tide!" and if a large company, "Rough sea!" By this means the number of those coming was made known. If the number was few, they were killed on the road; if a larger number, they were invited to the cave to eat and sleep, and large stones suspended above were dropped down on their heads where they were sitting, and thus they were killed. If the call was "Rough sea!" the travelers were allowed to go on their way.

One of the robbers was named Kapuaʻeuhi. He had two great, husky daughters who were his helpers. They had been taught the art of bone-breaking and wrestling and were just as good as men. They were also clever flatterers and decoys. At length, this robber band killed a certain young man of Ka'ū. The distressed family consulted a *kahuna,* and he advised them to send young kinsmen to destroy that band of robbers. [Two] kinsmen to the man who was killed went to 'Ōla'a, encountered the daughters of the robber, and began to wrestle with them. One man was almost overcome, but his loincloth loosened, and catching a corner of it in his hand, he wound it around the girl's neck and strangled her. He then helped his brother put to death the second girl. They hid the girls' bodies and went to the cave to await the father of the girls whom they had killed. When the old man saw them sitting at the entrance of the cave, he asked, "Where are my daughters?"

"Where indeed! We came by and stopped to rest."

"Come inside here," said the robber.

The young men looked up and, seeing the stones suspended, said, "No, thank you, we will sit here."

The old man suspected that they had killed his daughters, and he sprang upon them and attempted to kill them. There were two of them, and as he was a single man and aged, in the end they put him to death.

It is said that the plunder of these robbers is still in the cave of Kapua'euhi, but no one living knows how to move the stones to find the hidden cave.

The Hawaiian-language version of this story, *Nā 'Ōlohe o 'Ōla'a,* appears on page 145.

1. 'Ōlohe, a class of robbers who understand the art of bone-breaking. They pluck out all their hair and oil their bodies for wrestling in order to give no hold to an antagonist. Various places on the islands are known as the resorts of such robbers, and the story of the *'ōlohe* and his two daughters who act as decoys is told in other districts as well as in Ka'ū. For example, near the temple of Waha'ula, in Puna, the cave on the cliff is still pointed out where an *'ōlohe* and his daughters lived and terrorized the country. The daughters acted as lookout on the cliff, the *'ōlohe* descended to the sea path and hid. The daughters announced low or high tide, as in this story, and the *'ōlohe* dropped a tree trunk upon the passerby and crushed and robbed him. He kills a young man from Ka'ū named Kahele, and the man's father finally avenges his son's death upon the robber. A spot is shown on the shore road where the lava rock is twisted and torn as by a conflict, as the place where the father of Kahele fought with and killed the *'ōlohe.* See also Westervelt, *Gods and Ghosts,* 11. The *'ōlohe* may be represented as cannibals, as in the story of the *'ōlohe* of Hanakāpī'ai on Kaua'i (Fornander 5:210) or of Wahiawā on O'ahu (Dibble, *History...,* 113–115; Kalakaua, *Legends,* 371–380; Westervelt, *Legends of Old Honolulu,* 189–203; Thrum, *Folktales,* 139–146).

THE BLIND MEN OF MOA'ULA

In Moa'ula, Ka'ū, there were two men, one of whom was totally blind and the other of whom could only see things held close to his eyes. One day they started to go down to Punalu'u, the man who could see a little leading his totally blind companion. They went along slowly to the edge of the Punalu'u stream, and the blind man asked, "How is it? Is there water below?"

His companion answered, "Yes, there is water."

"Much water?"

"Yes, there is much water below."

"Then let us jump in and swim to the other side."

"Yes, let us jump in."

They jumped down and broke their legs. There was indeed water but not much.

Even this did not end their traveling together. One day the blind men went again to Punalu'u, but this time they approached the stream on the side toward the mountain. When they came to the stream, the completely blind man said to his guide, "What do you see? Is the water low?"

"Yes, very low."

"Is that true? Is there no water below?"

"It is true, there is no water."

"Then let us go down and wade across."

They went down, found the stream full of water, and were swept away. They were seen struggling in the water, dragged out, and taken home. Never again did they want to go to Punalu'u without someone who had good eyesight.

The Hawaiian-language version of this story, *Nā Makapō o Moa'ula*, appears on page 147.

HĀMAMALAU, OPEN LEAF

Hāmamalau, or Open Leaf, was a pretty woman, famed for her beauty from one end of the land to the other. A handsome man sought her for his wife and she consented. After the marriage, she returned with her husband to his part of the country. She was so pretty that her husband was very jealous of her. He built a house directly over a great pond and would not let his wife go away from the place. He came and went in a little canoe just big enough for himself, and when he went away, he made the door fast. At first when he went away, he returned every day, but by and by he went and forgot the woman living alone in the house. Every month he would go, return with food and fish, and go again and remain away a month. Thus he fed her. She ate the food he provided and waited quietly at home for his return.

Hāmamalau's family waited some time for their daughter to visit them and tell them how she was living. Becoming anxious, they sent her younger brother to inquire after her. Upon arriving, he met some friends of his brother-in-law and learned how his sister was kept close. The brother knew that Hāmamalau endured it because she loved her husband. He did not go at once to his sister's house but went instead to the friend of his sister's husband. There he planned her rescue. One very rainy night, he took a canoe and paddled to the door. The boy climbed up to the roof of the house, pulled out some of the thatch, very quietly unfastened the door and entered. He saw his sister sleeping in a corner and called, "Hāmamalau! My place here leaks; move over closer!" The girl thought that her husband had spoken, and she moved toward him. The brother moved away and called again, "Hāmamalau! My place here leaks, move over closer!" So the two moved along until they came to the door of the house, and the brother stepped into the canoe. It was a dark night and no stars were to be seen; Hāmamalau imagined that she was still in the house. When she moved again, she fell right into her brother's canoe. Swiftly he paddled to the sluice gates, lifted the canoe outside, and sailed away to their birthplace.

When Hāmamalau's parents saw her, they were full of pity. This woman who had gone away beautiful was now thin and sunken-eyed. They vowed that they would never let their daughter return to her unloving husband. When the husband went back to the house to find the wife, he heard how the brother had come for her, and he knew that if he went after Hāmamalau, he would be sent away because of his cruel treatment of her. Since he had no hope of recovering her, he took another wife.

The Hawaiian-language version of this story, *Hāmamalau*, appears on page 148.

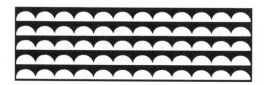

THE HOLE OF BLOOD

At Reid's Bay, Hilo, is a hole called Kaluakoko, the Hole of Blood. In ancient times, a man and his wife lived near that place. He was a fisherman and on calm days went fishing in his canoe. After a time, he met a woman of Keaukaha, and the two became fond of each other. The wife made no fuss when she heard of this and ordered her husband when he made a good catch to take some to the other woman. This went on for some years. One day, the husband turned to his wife and said, "My dear wife, it would be a good thing for your *punalua* to live with us, instead of my going fishing and taking her share to her and yours to you."[1] The wife answered, "That is a good plan. Fetch my *punalua* and bring her here, and we will live together." He fetched the woman of Keaukaha and brought her to live with them.

Strangely enough, it was the new wife who became jealous of the old, but she did not dare show her hatred. One day before going fishing, the husband forbade his wives to go fishing until his return.[2] As soon as the canoe had gone, the new wife said to her companion, "I say! The fish spawn must be thick on the beach; let us go catch it in a net."

The other answered, "No, our husband forbade us to go fishing. Let us stay in the house."

"Even so, let us go to the sea and catch shrimps and come right back." The *punalua* was so persistent that the other finally consented, and they went to catch shrimps. While the first wife was engaged in the shrimp catching and had come very close to the mouth of the hole, her *punalua* quickly shoved her in and covered the hole with a stone so that she could not get out. There she remained until she died. The new wife went home without the shrimps and with a dry fishnet so that it might not be known that she had gone to the beach.

At the wife's death, blood came out from her mouth and went on the sea foam to the place where the husband was fishing and encircled the canoe.[3] When he saw the blood, he thought of his wife and stopped fishing. He turned his canoe, and the blood went before him and guided the canoe to the hole. It made its way to the mouth of the hole and entered within. The husband moved the stone at the entrance and found the corpse of his wife. He carried it to a place near their house and hid it. Then seeing the other woman standing at the door of the house, he asked, "Where is your companion?"

The woman said, "I do not know. She asked me to go with her to catch shrimps, and when I would not go, she went alone with the net. She has not yet returned."

The man was furious. He said, "You are a lying woman. It is you who have murdered my dear wife. I loved her dearly. While I was fishing, her blood came to me and guided me to her." Then she was beaten to death by the husband. He took the first wife and hid her body in a burial cave. The second wife he left for her relatives to bury. The man did not return to live there again. It is for this reason that the hole is called the Hole of Blood, Kaluakoko.

The Hawaiian-language version of this story, *Kaluakoko,* appears on page 150. Told by Kaiama, a policeman who lived near Reid's Bay, about twenty years before this story was first published in 1936.

1. *Punalua* are the two husbands of one wife or the two wives of one husband. The relationship depends upon a custom whereby two sisters share a husband or two brothers a wife.

2. The conduct of the wife at home exerts an influence upon the husband's success in fishing, according to Hawaiian belief.

3. The blood signal is a motif very common in Samoan tales but not found, so far as I know, in old Hawaiian legend.

Pōhuehue

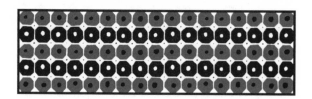

THE LAZY BEAUTY

One day, two girls went to dig sweet potatoes. When they had dug them, they took them under a pandanus tree to roast them. After the fire had been lighted, the lover of one of them appeared. The two climbed the pandanus tree to make love.

Periodically, the girl in the pandanus tree called down to the one below, "Say! Turn my potato!"

"Yes!" answered the girl below, and she turned her own potato without touching that of her companion. When her potato was thoroughly cooked, she ate it and put another on to roast.

The girl above called again, "Say! Did you turn my potato?" The other again answered that it was roasting.

When all her own potatoes were cooked and eaten, she went bathing in the sea. The girl in the pandanus tree suddenly thought of her potato and called again, "Say there! Turn my potato again." No one answered. She called again in a loud voice, "Turn my potato again!" No answer.

The two climbed down. The other girl's potatoes were gone; she had eaten them all up. Her own potatoes were either burned black in the fire or still raw. She was angry with her companion and, when she came back from bathing, scolded her well.

The second girl answered with a smile, "No lazy beauty for Ka'ū." With these words, she went off with her companion's lover. The man knew that if he had the lazy beauty for his wife, his potatoes would always be burned black in the fire.

The Hawaiian-language version of this story, *Ka U'i Palaualelo,* appears on page 152.

KAWELO THE SHOUTER

Kawelo was a woman famed for her beauty from one end of Ka'ū district to the other. She was so beautiful that her husband was dreadfully jealous whenever she spoke to other men.

One day, her husband saw her talking to one of their friends, and he was so angry that he killed Kawelo and placed her body in a cave situated on a point which jutted out into the ocean. Every day, when her husband went to fish, Kawelo's voice could be heard calling:

> O my husband, listen! You do not love me
> Or you would come to get me that we might go out
> fishing together.
> O my loveless husband, listen!

The man's fishing expeditions proved fruitless. So harassed and exasperated did he become because of her constant shouting that he took his wife's bones to the side of a blowhole on the seashore and pounded them to dust, muttering as he did so, "You have been able to call to me because your bones were not yet dust! Now there you are!" After powdering the bones, he left them lying where they had been crushed, and the sun scorched them until they were bleached. When the tide rose through the blowhole, they were washed inside the hole and lost in its depths.[1] But still could her voice be heard from the depths calling,

> O my husband, listen! You do not love me
> Or you would come and take me fishing with you!

Her husband could not possibly do as she wished, for it meant certain death to plunge into the blowhole. The only thing he could do was to stifle his wrath.

The woman continued to call in this manner until her husband's death. After that time, her voice predicted strange events that were to befall the land and thus foretold to the natives of that locality what events were to be expected. When Kamehameha became the ruling monarch, Kawelo's voice was heard from within the blowhole calling, "Another country shall possess the land! Another country shall possess the land!"

The men who heard her thus shouting answered, "O Kawelo! Kamehameha possesses the land, one of our own sons of Hawai'i here."[2]

But the voice answered, "Not so! The land shall not be for Pai'ea, it shall belong to the sea. Another country will possess the land!"

Her cry was heard from Paepae, where the blowhole lies, below the precipice of Pōhina, to the villages of Pāhala and of Kahuku, so that it became the chief subject of conversation among the people of that vicinity.

Her cry did not cease until after the annexation treaty of this fine land with the United States.[3] After the death of Kamehameha, the cry continued: "Another country shall possess the land!"[4] Dwellers in that part of the island have said that when the arrangements were being made to take Hawai'i as a part of the United States of America, the prophecy of Kawelo was heard, "O my nation, listen! Annexation! Annexation! Another country shall possess the land."

Since that time, some mischievous visitors to the spot have broken away the mouth of the blowhole, leaving a great gap. Kawelo still calls, but the opening is so large that her words cannot be plainly understood. Only those who are near can hear what is said; people at a distance hear the voice, but the words are lost.

Because of this voice, the blowhole bears the name of Kawelo, Kawelo the Shouter.

The Hawaiian-language version of this story, *Kawelohea,* appears on page 155. This story was told by Mrs. Wiggin.

1. Legend often gathers about the phenomenon of a spouting horn in Hawai'i.

2. The word used here, Pai'ea, is a familiar name of Kamehameha I.

3. This happened in 1898.

4. In 1819. [Ed.]

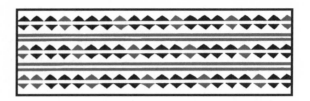

MŌLĪ'S LEAP

Among all the handsome women of that period, none excelled Mōlī. Many suitors appeared, but her father refused them all, saying that he would bestow his daughter only upon a skillful fisherman.

There was a certain worthless, red-eyed fellow who heard what the father had said, and he began to seek means by which he could possess Mōlī. So he ate quantities of shellfish and rubbed his skin with shellfish and the intestines of fish (which others threw away) until he had a strong fishy odor. Then he went to Mōlī's father to ask for this beautiful woman. The father, smelling the fishy stench from the red-eyed man and thinking, "This is a genuine fisherman!" immediately consented, and within a few days the marriage took place.

But the provoking thing was that all this man cared to do was to sleep. When Mōlī had prepared the food, he moved forward to eat; when he had done, he slept. At last, his wife's endurance was at an end, and she threw herself over the precipice which is today called "Mōlī's Leap." It is situated at Wai'ahukini, in the district of Ka'ū, near South Point.

Before leaping to her death over the precipice that now bears her name, Mōlī adorned herself with *lei* of wild ginger, fern, and *maile*. Once a year, on the anniversary of her death, she returns to the scene of the tragedy. Winds blow, and in them one can hear moaning and shrieking. Woe befalls anyone who at any time wears a *maile lei* at Mōlī's Leap, for Mōlī will knock the wearer prostrate to the ground. In fact, the wind plays strange tricks at Mōlī's Leap. Any light object such as a hat or twig is often blown out to sea and then blown back to dash against the cliff. Small plants which cling to the soil are often twisted into strange shapes or uprooted and cast into the sea below.

Told with additional notes by Mary Kawena Pukui from the story as given by her mother's cousin, Mrs. Keli'ihue Alakaihu of Ka'ū.

THE MISCHIEVOUS SUN

Kalākolohe, the Mischievous Sun, was a famous *kahuna* of Ka'ū. He was not a priest who took life but one who understood healing, a reader of the signs in the clouds.[1] The sun was one of his gods. At Honokāne gulch was a *heiau* which had been kept by his ancestors up to the time when such things were abolished.[2]

Mr. Hutchinson, of the Hutchinson Sugar Plantation company, was the head of the sugar plantation adjoining the place where Kalākolohe lived. Among the Hawaiians of Ka'ū, he was known as Palapoi, Dried Poi. The reason for this name was that his neck was burned to a crisp in the sun, and the skin peeled off like dried poi.

Mr. Hutchinson often heard of Kalākolohe's power and of his ability always to obtain what he prayed for, so when the land got too dry, he went to the *kahuna* and asked him to be so kind as to pray for rain. The *kahuna* prayed, rain fell, and everything grew well. The next time that the cane and the grass in the fields grew dry, Mr. Hutchinson again went to the *kahuna* to pray for rain. He got what he wanted. Finally, the *kahuna* grew vexed with the white man's constant appeals to him to pray for rain, and he prayed for a downpour. Day and night it rained, until Mr. Hutchinson went and asked him to stop the rain. With the return of the dry season, the grass again became parched. The animals had no water. Hutchinson went again to Kalākolohe to ask for rain. As before, the rain did not cease, so the white man went again to the *kahuna* to cause it to cease. This went on for a long time.

One day, Hutchinson went to Kalākolohe and asked for rain. The *kahuna* was by this time thoroughly vexed, so he asked, "Palapoi, do you want rain very much?"

"Yes, I want it badly. The sugarcane is getting dry."

"If you want the rain very much, take your gun and shoot the seat of the sun's pants." And with these words, the *kahuna* went into the house, leaving the white man standing outside, the image of disappointment.

That night the knowledge came to the *kahuna* in his sleep that he had not long to live because of his angry words about shooting his god, the sun, in the seat of the pants. He rose and awakened his family and told them that he was to die because of his insulting words to his god. The

103

next day, it was learned that he was dead. Many people went to see their powerful *kahuna*.

The *heiau* of Honokāne is destroyed, all but the foundations. It is said that in this gulch the tumult of joyful chanting and confused shouting may be heard, although no one is to be seen there. Within this gulch the *kukui* tree, *noni* apple, mango, orange, *hau* tree, coconut, pandanus, and fig flourish, with many other kinds of trees besides. From ancient times to the time of Kalākolohe, a strict taboo protected this fruit, but since his death, the people all go and help themselves to it.

The Hawaiian-language version of this story, *Kalākolohe*, appears on page 157.

1. A *kahuna* who read signs in the clouds was called a *kahuna kilokilo*. A worshiper of Lā, the Sun, was supposed to have control over rain. The drought that came in the days of Hua, king of East Maui, in answer to the prayer of a priest he had slain, has become proverbial in Hawai'i. See Kalakaua, *Legends*, 157–173.

2. Honokāne gulch was once the site of a temple of the sun. At the time of this story, it was in ruins, although the priest still lived there and worshiped the sun.

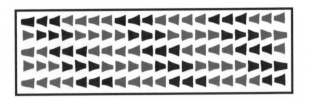

KĀNE A ME KŪ

He kaʻao kēia no kekahi ʻelemakule o Hilo i ke au kahiko loa. He kanaka ia i hoʻomaopopo mau i kona mau akua, iā Kane a me Kū. I kona ala ʻana i kakahiaka, ʻōlelo aʻela ia, "E Kāne ē, e Kū ē, ua ala au!" A i ka wā ona e hoʻomoʻa ai i kāna wahi mea e pāʻina ai, hea akula ia, "E Kāne, e Kū, e hoomoʻa ana au i kuʻu mea ʻai." A i ka moʻa ʻana, kono akula ʻo ia iā lāua, me ka ʻī ʻana, "E Kāne ē, e Kū ē, ua moʻa ka ʻai, a e ʻai ana au, mai kākou e pāʻina!" A hiki i ka wā e māʻona ai, ʻōlelo hou aʻela nō ia, "E Kāne ē, e Kū ē, ua māʻona au!" Kiʻi aʻela ia i ka ʻōʻō no ka hele ʻana e mahi i kāna māla ʻuala, hea hou akula nō ʻo ia i ua mau akua nei, "E Kāne, e Kū, e hele ana au e mahi ʻai. E hele pū kākou." Pēia ʻo ia i hea mau ai i kona mau akua i nā mea a pau āna i hana ai.

I kekahi lā, hele aku nei ʻo ia me kekahi mau hoa i kahakai no ka lawe iʻa. Hihia iho nei ka ʻupena i kekahi ʻākoʻakoʻa i loko o ke kai. Hea aʻe nei ʻo ia iā Kāne a me Kū me ka ʻī ʻana, "E luʻu ana au e wehe i ka ʻupena," a luʻu akula. Kakali aku nei kona mau hoa no ke aea aʻe, ʻaʻole naʻe i ʻōʻili mai ua ʻelemakule nei. No laila i manaʻo ai lākou ua make, a hoʻi akula e haʻi i ka ʻohana, ua make ka ʻelemakule i loko o ke kai.

I ua ʻelemakule nei i luʻu aku ai, nalowale aʻela ua ʻākoʻakoʻa nei, me ka ʻupena, a kau aʻela ʻo ia i luna o kekahi ʻāina maikaʻi. ʻĪ ihola ia, "E Kāne, e Kū, nani maoli kēia ʻāina! E ʻimi ana au i nā kamaʻāina o kēia wahi." Hele aʻela ʻo ia a ʻike akula i kekahi hale pili e kū ana, a lohe aku nei ʻo ia i ka leo e hea mai ana iā ia e hele aku. Auau akula ʻo ia me ka ʻoliʻoli, a ʻōlelo aʻela ia, "E Kāne, e Kū, ke hea maila kamaʻāina iaʻu, a e hele ana au i laila!"

I kona puka ʻana i ka hale, ʻike akula ia he ʻelua mau ʻelemakule. Hoʻokipa ʻia ʻo ia me ka maikaʻi. Moe ihola ia i laila i kēlā pō. I ke ao ʻana aʻe, ʻī maila kekahi ʻelemakule iā ia, "ʻEa, ua lohe mau māua i kou hea mau i ko māua inoa. ʻO wau nō ʻo Kāne, a ʻo kēia ʻo Kū. Ke mahalo nei māua i kou hea ʻole iā māua i kou hele ʻana i hoʻopau pilikia. Akā, e puka mau ana ko māua inoa no nā mea a pau, a ua uluhua nō hoʻi māua. No laila māua i lawe mai ai iā ʻoe e aʻo aku ai māua. Ala ʻoe, hoʻomanaʻo, a ke pilikia, hea mai, a ke moe, noʻonoʻo mai. Ō hoʻi, a ka wā pono, kiʻi aku māua iā ʻoe."

Hoʻihoʻi ʻia maila ua kanaka nei i kona wahi ponoʻī. ʻOliʻoli nā makamaka i ka ʻike hou ʻana i kona mau maka, a me ka lohe ʻana i ka ʻāina nani āna i ʻike ai. Mau makahiki lōʻihi ma hope mai, nalowale ua kanaka nei. Ua ʻōlelo ʻia, ua hoʻi ʻo ia e noho me kona mau akua, me Kāne a me Kū.

The English-language version of this story, *Kāne and Kū*, appears on page 11.

NĀ WILIWILI O PĀʻULA

He ʻehā ko lākou nui i hānau ʻia mai ai e ko lākou makuahine. ʻO Moholani ka hiapo, ʻo Wiliwiliʻoheʻohe mai, ʻo Wiliwilipeʻapeʻa, a ʻo Wiliwilikuapuʻu nō hoʻi ko lākou muli loa. ʻO Moholani ka uʻi o lākou a pau. He uʻi nō ʻo Wiliwiliʻoheʻohe, ʻo ka ʻōhule naʻe. He uʻi nō hoʻi ʻo Wiliwilipeʻapeʻa a ʻo ka ʻōpeʻapeʻa hoʻi ʻo kona ʻano. Ke puhi mai ka makani, e kīlepalepa wale ana nō kona lauoho ma ʻō a ma ʻaneʻi. Ma kona inoa nō hoʻi kākou e hoʻomaopopo ai he uʻi kuapuʻu ʻo Wiliwilikuapuʻu.

ʻO Moholani wale nō ka mea i hoʻāo ʻia me ke kāne, a hoʻokahi a lāua keiki, ʻo Kauilamākēhāokalani. Ua hoʻihoʻi ʻia ʻo Kauilamākēhāokalani me nā akua o lākou e hānai ʻia ai i Kuaihelani, ka ʻāina huna i ke ao.

I ka hele mau o ke kāne a Moholani i ka lae kahakai, ʻike mai nei kekahi mau wāhine kupua o ke kai i ka uʻi o kēia kanaka. ʻO ko lāua hoʻohihi nō ia. ʻO ʻAhikananā ka inoa o kekahi wahine, a ʻo ʻAhikāhuli hoʻi kekahi. I nā wā a pau e hoʻowalewale mau ana lāua i ke kāne a Moholani, ma ke oli ʻana i nā mele o ke kai, a ka haʻi ʻana nō hoʻi i nā kaʻao o ka moana kūlipolipo. Hele iho nei ua kanaka nei a puni iā lāua lā; ʻo ka luʻu nō ia i loko o ke kai, a hoʻi pū me lāua i ko lāua ana i ka papakū o ka moana.

Kakali mai ʻo Moholani, a ʻo ka hoʻi ʻole aku o ke kāne, ʻimi nei i nā wahi a pau āna i ʻike ai. Ua haʻi mai kekahi poʻe i ʻike ua lilo iā ʻAhikananā a me ʻAhikāhuli. Iā ia i kokoke mai ai i kahi o ke kaikaina e noho ana, hea mai nei ʻo ia, "E Wiliwiliʻoheʻohe ē! Kū mai nei ē! E Wiliwili-ʻoheʻohe ē! Kū mai nei ē! Ua ʻike paha ʻoe i kuʻu kāne i lawe ʻia e ʻAhikananā, e ʻAhikāhuli? ʻIliʻili pekepeke, ʻiliʻili nehe!" Nānā mai nei ʻo Wiliwiliʻoheʻohe, a pane mai nei me ke keu, "ʻĒ! Kāne nui palaualelo! ʻAʻohe au i ʻike i kāu kāne!"

Hele aku nei nō ʻo Moholani me ka hāloʻiloʻi o kona waimaka i ka lua o ke kaikaina, a hea maila, "E Wiliwilipeʻapeʻa ē! Kū mai nei ē! E Wiliwilipeʻapeʻa ē! Kū mai nei ē! Ua ʻike paha ʻoe i kuʻu kāne i lawe ʻia e ʻAhikananā, e ʻAhikāhuli? ʻIliʻili pekepeke, ʻiliʻili nehe!" Ua like nō kā Wiliwilipeʻapeʻa pane me kā kona mua aʻe. "ʻĒ! Kāne nui palaualelo! ʻO wai ka mea i ʻike i kāu kāne!"

Hoʻomau aku nei ʻo Moholani i ka hele ʻana a kahi o ko lākou muli loa, a hea maila e like nō me kāna i hea mua ai. ʻAʻohe nō hoʻi i ʻokoʻa ka pane a Wiliwilikuapuʻu mai kā nā kaikuaʻana mai, "ʻĒ! Kāne nui palaualelo! ʻAʻohe au i ʻike iā ia!"

No ka ʻike o Moholani i ke aloha ʻole o nā pōkiʻi, hea aku nei i ke keiki, me ke kaukau pū i nā kahu hānai akua o ke keiki e hoʻokuʻu mai iā ia. Ua hele maila ʻo Kauilamākēhāokalani, a i ka lohe ʻana i ke kaukau o kona makuahine iā ia, hele aku nei ʻo ia e kiʻi i ka makua kāne e hoʻi mai. ʻAʻole i ʻae ʻo ʻAhikananā lāua ʻo ʻAhikāhuli e hoʻokuʻu i ka ipo o lāua.

No ko lāua ʻauʻa loa, piʻi aʻe nei ka huhū o Kauilamākēhāokalani. Loli aʻe nei ke kino kanaka ona a ke kino uila. I ka ʻoaka ʻana o ka uila i ka papakū o ka moana, ua ʻokiʻoki ʻia ua mau wāhine nei a paukūkū. Lilo aʻe nei nā paukū i iʻa, a mai laila mai i loaʻa ai kēlā ʻano iʻa, he ʻahi. Pau ka hiki ʻana o ua mau wāhine nei e hoʻowalewale i kā haʻi kāne, ʻoiai ua lilo loa aʻela i iʻa!

No ke aloha ʻole o nā kaikaina iā Moholani, ua hoʻolilo ʻia lākou i mau kumu wiliwili. No ka ʻōhule o Wiliwiliʻoheʻohe, ua lilo ʻo ia i kumu lāʻau māʻoheʻohe lau ʻole. ʻO ko Wiliwilipeʻapeʻa mau lau e kīlepalepa mau ana i ke aheahe a ka makani. E like nō me ke kuapuʻu o Wiliwilikuapuʻu, pēia nō ke kekeʻe o kona kumu. ʻAʻole i hele ʻauana hou ke kāne a Moholani, no ka mea ua ʻike ʻo ia he keiki hoʻoponopono ʻole kāna ke huhū iho.

The English-language version of this story, *The Wiliwili Trees of Pāʻula*, appears on page 13.

Ma'o

KŪKAʻŌHIʻAAKALAKA

ʻO Kūkaʻōhiʻaakalaka ke kaikunāne a ʻo Kauakuahine ke kaikuahine. Mai Kahiki mai lāua a noho i Hawaiʻi, ʻo Kauakuahine i ʻŌlaʻa me kāna kāne, a ʻo Kūkaʻōhiʻaakalaka i Keaʻau me kāna wahine. ʻAʻohe keiki a Kūkaʻōhiʻaakalaka, a ʻo ke kaikuahine hoʻi, he mau keiki nō. He mahi ʻai ka hana a ke kaikuahine i ʻŌlaʻa a he lawaiʻa kā ke kaikunāne i Keaʻau.

I kēlā a me kēia manawa, ua iho ʻo Kauakuahine me ka ʻai i kahakai na ke kaikunāne a ʻo ka iʻa kāna e hoʻihoʻi mai ai na kona ʻohana. Ua kauoha ʻo Kūkaʻōhiʻaakalaka i kāna wahine e hāʻawi a nui i ka iʻa maloʻo i kona kaikuahine i nā wā a pau āna e iho mai ai me ka ʻai. Ua nānā ihola ka wahine i ka iʻa maloʻo a minamina, a hoʻihoʻi aku nei ma lalo o nā moena e hūnā ai.

I ka iho ʻana mai o Kauakuahine me ka ʻai, ua hala ke kaikunāne i ka lawaiʻa. ʻŌlelo aku nei ke kaikoʻeke, "ʻAʻohe iʻa a māua lā. E nānā aʻe nō ʻoe i kauhale nei, ua nele. ʻO ka paʻakai wale nō kahi mea i loaʻa." Hele nō ʻo Kauakuahine a loaʻa ka līpahapaha, ʻo ko iala hoʻi nō ia. I ka iho hou ʻana mai o Kauakuahine, ʻo ia ana nō, ʻo ka hoʻi nō me ka nele. I ahona nō i kahi līpahapaha.

No ka pī mau o ke kaikoʻeke, ua lilo ia i mea hoʻokaumaha iā Kauakuahine. I kekahi hoʻi ʻana āna me ka līpahapaha, ua manaʻo ʻo ia he mea makehewa ka hoʻoluhi ʻana iā ia iho e lawe mau aku i ka ʻai i Keaʻau a ʻo ka līpahapaha wale nō ka iʻa e hoʻihoʻi aku ai na kāna kāne hoʻomanawanui a me nā keiki a lāua.

I ke kokoke ʻana aku ona i ka hale o lākou ua holo maila ke kāne a me nā keiki e ʻike iā ia. Ua paʻipaʻi pākahi akula ʻo ia iā lākou a lilo lākou i mau ʻiole. ʻO ka ʻiole māhuahua, ka makua kāne ia; ʻo nā ʻiole makaliʻi, ʻo nā keiki nō ia. No Kauakuahine, ua lilo ʻo ia i pūnāwai me ka ua kilihune e heleleʻi ana ma laila.

I ke kaikunāne e lawaiʻa ana, ua hiki akula ka hōʻike a nā akua iā ia i ke pī o ka wahine i ka iʻa a i ka lilo o ke kaikuahine i wai a ʻo ka ʻohana i pua

111

'iole. Ua lilo kēia i mea kaumaha i kona noʻonoʻo a hoʻi aku nei i kauhale a nīnau aku i ka wahine, "Ua hāʻawi anei ʻoe i iʻa na nā pōkiʻi o kāua?" "ʻAe, ke hāʻawi mau nei nō au i ka iʻa."

ʻO ko Kūkaʻōhiʻaakalaka lālau akula nō ia i nā moena o ka hale o lāua a hāpai aʻela i luna. ʻIke aʻela ʻo ia i nā iʻa maloʻo, ua hoʻonoho papa ʻia ma lalo aʻe o ka moena, a e hoholo aʻe ana nā puʻu. Ua piha loa ʻo ia i ka inaina, a ʻī aku nei i ka wahine, "He keu ʻoe a ka wahine loko ʻino. Pōʻino kuʻu pōkiʻi iā ʻoe." A me kēia mau hua ʻōlelo ua pepehi ʻia kēlā wahine a make loa.

Ua piʻi akula ʻo ia i ʻŌlaʻa i kahi a ke kaikuahine a ʻike aku nei ʻo ia i ka hoholo mai o nā ʻiole i kauhale a kulu iho nei kona waimaka aloha no ke kaikoʻeke a me nā keiki. Hele pololei aku nei ʻo ia a ka pūnāwai a iho iho nei ke poʻo i lalo i loko o ka wai, a ʻo ke kino, ua lilo aʻela i kumu ʻōhiʻa.

He ʻelua wale nō pua o kēia kumu ʻōhiʻa i nā wā a pau, a ke haki ka lālā, kahe mai ke koko mai kona kino mai.

The English-language version of this story, *Kūkaʻōhiʻaakalaka* appears on page 19.

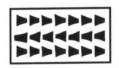

KA MOʻOLELO O PŌHAKUOHANALEI
A ME PŌHAKUOLĒKIA

I ka hele ʻana mai o Pele a me kona ʻohana mai Kahiki mai, ʻo ka Pōhakuohanalei, Pōhakuolēkia, Pōhakuokua, Pōhakuomālei, Pōhakuokaʻa, Pōhakuokāne, Pōhakuloa a me Pōhakuolono kekahi i hele pū mai me lākou i nā moku o Hawaiʻi nei.

Noho ʻo Pōhakuohanalei i Kauaʻi, a ʻo Pōhakuolēkia i Kapoho, Puna, a ʻo Pōhakuokua a me ka Pōhakuolono i Kaʻū, Hawaiʻi. ʻO Pōhakuloa i ʻŌlaʻa, Hawaiʻi, a ma hope mai ʻo ia i hele hou mai ai i ka mokupuni ʻo Oʻahu. A ʻo ka Pōhakumālei hoʻi, i Makapuʻu, Oʻahu. ʻO ka Pōhakuokaʻa, he pōhaku kakaʻa ia ma nā wahi āna e makemake ai. No laila, ua hiki ʻole ke hōʻike akāka ʻia kona wahi noho paʻa. A i Kona i noho ai ka Pōhakuokāne. ʻO kēia moʻolelo, no ka Pōhakuohanalei a me ka Pōhakuolēkia.

I ka hele ʻana o Pele a noho paʻa i nā kuahiwi o Hawaiʻi, hū aʻela kona aloha iā Pōhakuohanalei e noho ana ma Kauaʻi; no laila, kiʻi aku nei ʻo ia iā ia e hoʻi aʻe ma kona wahi noho ma Hawaiʻi. Hoʻi aku nei ka Pōhakuohanalei a noho pū me Pele a me kona ʻohana i luna o Mokuʻāweoweo.

I kekahi manawa nō hoʻi, hele lākou i Puna i ka ʻauʻau kai, ka heʻe hōlua, a me nā leʻaleʻa ʻē aʻe o ia wā. I nā wahi a lākou e hele ai i nā leʻaleʻa, ʻo ka Pōhakuolēkia kekahi i hele pū me lākou. No ka hoʻohihi o ka Pōhakuolēkia i ka uʻi o ka Pōhakuohanalei, noi aku nei ʻo ia iā Pele e ʻae mai i ko lāua hoʻāo. ʻIke aku nei ʻo Pele i ko lāua makemake loa o kekahi i kekahi a hāʻawi maila ʻo ia i kona ʻae.

I ko lāua hoʻāo ʻana, hoʻi aku nei lāua i kahi o ka Pōhakuolēkia i wae ai i home no lāua. Eia nō lāua ke kū nei ma kēlā puʻu a hiki i kēia lā. ʻO ka moʻolelo o lāua me ke kupua Kālaikini, he moʻolelo ia i kamaʻāina i ko Puna poʻe.

The English-language version of this story, *The Rock of Hanalei and the Rock of Lēkia,* appears on page 21.

113

I kekahi mau kaikamāhine e pūlehu ʻulu ana i ke kula, ua kaena aʻe nei lāua i ko lāua mau akua. ʻĪ aʻe nei kekahi, "ʻO Laka koʻu akua, he akua maikaʻi." ʻŌlelo maila hoʻi kona kōkoʻolua, "ʻO Kapo koʻu akua, he akua ʻoluʻolu."

Iā lāua e nanea ana i ke kaena i ko lāua akua, ua ʻōʻili maila he luahine. ʻĪ maila ia i ke kaikamahine mua,

"Naʻu hoʻi kahi ʻulu āu."

"ʻAʻole," i pane mai ai ke kaikamahine, "na Laka kaʻu ʻulu."

"He akua mana nō anei ʻo Laka?"

"ʻAe, he akua mana nō."

"Naʻu hoʻi kekahi wai o kāu hue wai."

"ʻAʻole nō; na Laka nō kēia wai."

A huli mai nei ka luahine i ka lua o ke kaikamahine a noi mai nei i ka ʻulu. Ua ʻike nō kēlā kaikamahine, ʻaʻohe ʻo ia i hoʻohiki i kāna ʻulu na kona akua punahele a no laila, ua hāʻawi maila ʻo ia i kāna ʻulu me ka ʻoluʻolu. I ka pau ʻana o ka ʻai ʻana a ka luahine, ua noi maila ʻo ia i ka wai o kāna hue wai, a ua loaʻa aku nō.

ʻEu aʻe nei ua luahine nei e hele, a ma mua o kona hele loa ʻana, ʻōlelo maila ʻo ia i ka mea i hāʻawi lokomaikaʻi aku i ka ʻulu iā ia, "Ō hoʻi a hōʻike aku i kou mau mākua e hoʻolako i ka hale i ka ʻai a lawa, a e kau i ka lepa i nā kihi pā ma mua o ka hala ʻana o ke anahulu." I ka hōʻike ʻana aku o kēia kaikamahine i kēia mea i kona ʻohana, ua ʻike koke maila lākou, ʻaʻole kēia he wahine ʻē, ʻo Pele nō. A ua hauʻoli nō hoʻi lākou i ka lokomaikaʻi o ke kaikamahine iā ia.

Ua hoʻokō ʻia nā kauoha a pau a i ka piha ʻana o ka ʻumi lā, ua ʻike ʻia ka ʻā o ka pele i luna o Mokuʻāweoweo. Ua kahe ka pele i Kaʻū a ua pau kekahi poʻe hale i ka luku ʻia a koe nō ka hale a me ka ʻohana o ke kaika-mahine lokomaikaʻi.

Ua aʻo mau nā mākua a me nā kūpuna i kā lākou mau pulapula ʻaʻole e pī, ʻaʻole hoʻi e pane kīkoʻolā i nā malihini, o hiki mai auaneʻi ka lā e pane kū ʻia ai ʻo Pele ke hele mai ʻo ia, a pōʻino lākou.

The English-language version of this story, entitled *The Breadfruit Offering,* appears on page 23.

MAKANIKEOE, KE AKUA O KE ALOHA

Hele mai 'o Makanikeoe me kona kaikuahine, me Lauka'ie'ie, a hiki i Puna. No Kahiki mai lāua. A 'ī akula kekahi i kekahi, "E hele 'oe i kou alanui, a e hele nō au i ko'u." A i ia wā i 'ike ai 'o Makanikeoe i ka waha o kekahi ana. Komo aku 'o ia i loko, a hele aku nei i loko o nā lua huna, a puka aku nei 'o ia i ke kuahiwi.

Ua 'ike aku 'o ia i kekahi kanaka e uē ana. Ma muli o kona kūlana akua, ua ho'omaopopo 'o ia iā Kānekoa. 'Ī aku nei 'o ia, "E Kānekoa, e aha ana 'oe ma 'ane'i?" Pane mai 'o Kānekoa, "I hele mai ho'i au no ke kipaku 'ana mai nei ia'u e ku'u mau mākua hūnōai, a ua kā'ili 'ia aku nei ku'u wahine."

'Aka'aka ihola 'o Makanikeoe; nīnau maila 'o ia, "No ke aha 'oe i kipaku 'ia mai nei?" Pane mai 'o Kānekoa, "Ua 'ōlelo mai nei ku'u makua hūnōai wahine he kanaka palaualelo wau. 'O ka mahi 'ai nō, a ho'omaha, he palaualelo ia; mai ka lawe i'a mai nō, a ho'omaha, 'o ka palaualelo nō ia. Makemake nō ku'u makua hūnōai e mahi 'ai a lawe i'a nō wau a pō ka lā, me ke ku'u 'ole i ka luhi."

'Ī mai nei 'o Makanikeoe, "E hele mai kāua i ku'u ana, a i laila kāua e noho ai. E lilo nō ho'i 'oe i aikāne aloha na'u. A e ho'olohe mai 'oe i ka'u mau 'ōlelo a'o iā 'oe." A i ko lāua ho'i 'ana i ke ana, ulu ka mai'a, ka 'awa, ke kalo, ka 'uala a me ka uhi i ko lākou 'ike 'ana i ke akua.

Hele nō lāua i ka lawe i'a i Puna, a ho'i mai nō ma loko mai o ke ana. 'Ōlelo nō 'o Makanikeoe i kona kōko'olua, "E ku'i 'oe i ka 'ai a nui, a laila pi'i i kapa alanui, a 'o ka po'e e hele ana, kāhea aku e 'ai." Ho'okō nō 'o Kānekoa, a 'o ka po'e hele o ke alanui, e lohe mau ana lākou i ka leo kāhea o Kānekoa, "Mai e 'ai, mai e 'ai!" A 'o ka po'e pōloli, iho i loko o ke ana e 'ai ai. Ho'i kekahi po'e i Ka'ū, ha'i mai lākou i kēia nūhou 'ano 'ē no Kānekoa.

I ia mau lā, e ho'omākaukau ana nā mākua hūnōai o Kānekoa e 'imi i kāne aku no kāna wahine. Lohe iho nei lākou no Kānekoa, a pi'i a nui ka huhū o nā mākua hūnōai a me ka hūnōna hou. Ho'omākaukau lākou no ka hele aku i 'Ōla'a e pepehi iā Kānekoa.

ʻIke iho nei ʻo Makanikeoe, a ʻōlelo aku nei ʻo ia iā Kānekoa, "E hoʻolilo aʻe au iaʻu iho i kumu lāʻau, a kū i ka puka o ke ana, a i hele mai ka ʻohana o kāu wahine, e holo mai ʻoe a hehi i kuʻu kino." ʻAkahi ʻo Kānekoa a ʻike he aikāne akua kona.

Hele aku nei ʻo Kānekoa i kapa alanui e like me ka mea maʻa mau iā ia; ʻike aku nei ʻo ia i ka ʻohana o ka wahine e hele mai ana. Nuku mai nei ka makua hūnōai wahine, a holo mai nei ka hūnōna hou me ka paukū lāʻau e pepehi iā Kānekoa.

Holo aku nei ʻo Kānekoa a hiki i ka waha o ke ana a hehi aku nei i ke kumu lāʻau. ʻIke ʻo ia i kona kuʻu mālie ʻana i lalo. Lilo aʻe nei ke kino lāʻau o Makanikeoe i kino kanaka a kāhea aku nei me ka leo nui, "E hāpuʻu ē!" A pane mai nei nā kumu hāpuʻu, "Eō! Eō!" Hea aku nei ʻo ia, "E ʻōhiʻa ē! E maile ē! E pala ē! E uluhe ē! E hōʻiʻo ē! E ʻākōlea ē! E ʻamaʻu ē! E palaʻā ē! E kikawaiō ē! E ʻēkaha ē! E pohepohe ē!" A hea pākahi aku nei ʻo ia i ka inoa o ka nahele o ke kuahiwi. Pane mai nei lākou a pau, "Eō! Eō!"

I ka lohe ʻana o nā mākua hūnōai a me ka punalua o Kānekoa i kēia mau mea, piha nei lākou me ka makaʻu, kiola nei lākou i kā lākou mau lāʻau a holo. Ua manaʻo kēia poʻe he kupua me nā menehune ka mea i walaʻau mai.

ʻIke iho nei ʻo Makanikeoe e hiki mai ana ka wī ma Kaʻū, a ʻōlelo aku nei ʻo ia i kona hoa, "Inā e hele mai kāu wahine, e hāʻawi aku ʻoe; a inā ʻo ka ʻohana o kāu wahine, a laila, e kipaku aku, ʻoiai ua ʻī mai lākou he palaualelo ʻoe, malia ua hiki ʻole ke ʻai i kāu ʻai." ʻĪ aku nei ʻo Kānekoa, "Inā e uē loa mai, e aloha aku nei paha." ʻŌlelo mai nei ʻo Makanikeoe, "E kipaku aku, a na ke au nō e ʻike aku ko mua."

Ma hope, wī ʻiʻo nei nō ʻo Kaʻū, a nui ka poʻe i hele i ke ana o Kānekoa mā e kiʻi i ʻai na lākou. Hoʻi aku nei lākou i Kaʻū, a haʻi aku i ko laila poʻe, "He nui ka ʻai a Kānekoa." Lohe iho nei ka wahine a Kānekoa, hele aku nei ʻo ia me ka uē i ka makuahine a ʻī aku nei, "Kipaku ʻoe i kuʻu kāne, iā Kānekoa, ka mea nui o ka ʻai a makemake iho nei ʻoe e hoʻāo wau me kēia kāne hou, a laila, ʻike ihola ka ʻōpū i ka pōloli!"

I ia manawa, ua hoʻomākaukau nā mākua me ke kāne a me ka ʻohana e hele iā Kānekoa. I ka hiki ʻana aku i ke ana, e kū mai ana ke kino kumu lāʻau o Makanikeoe i ka puka o ka lua.

Makaʻu ʻo Kānekoa i ka hoʻokuli i kona aikāne, no laila, kiʻi aku nei ʻo ia i ka wahine e hoʻihoʻi i lalo o ka lua e hānai ai. Noho mai nā mākua me

ka ʻohana ma luna a pōloli loa. Hoʻāʻo lākou e hele mai a komo i loko o
ka lua, akā, i ke kokoke ʻana e komo, niniu aʻe nei ua kumu lāʻau nei, a ua
hoʻokuʻi ʻia lākou e nā lālā. Holo aku nei lākou i kahi ʻē loa a noho mai e
kakali i ka wahine a Kānekoa. I ka māʻona ʻana o kēlā wahine, ʻo ka hoʻi
nō ia o lākou no Kaʻū.

Kekahi mau lā mai, ʻī aku ua kaikamahine nei i kona makuahine, "ua
hele mai nei kā hoʻi ka ʻai a Kānekoa a kau i ka maka! E ʻoluʻolu ʻoe e hele
au i kahi mau lā i ka lae kahakai e hoʻohulihuli pōhaku ai, malia e loaʻa ai
kahi ʻaʻama e ʻai aʻe ai kākou." Mea mai nei ka makuahine, "Ō hele ia; ua
hele mai nei kēia a nāwaliwali i ka pōloli." Hele pololei ua kaikamahine
nei i kahi o ke kāne; ʻo ka ʻai nō ia a māʻona, hoʻi. Haʻi aku nei i ka
makuahine, "ʻAʻohe ʻaʻama o kahakai." ʻO ka mea kupanaha i ʻike ʻia,
wīwī ka ʻohana, momona ka wahine!

No ka pilikia loa, hele hou aku nei nā mākua i kahi o Kānekoa a uē
aku, "Auē! Ke keiki maikaʻi! Ka mea hānai i ka makua! He ʻai nō i kou
noho mai—hele aʻe, pōloli mākou!"

ʻAʻole i ʻike kēia poʻe e kū mai ana ʻo Makanikeoe i mua o lākou.
Pūʻiwa lākou i ka lohe ʻana i kekahi leo e ʻī mai ana, "E ʻai nō i ka ʻai a
Kānekoa, ke hana i ka mea pololei. E hoʻihoʻi mai i kā Kānekoa wahine
me ia, a e kipaku i ke kāne hou. E noho nō ʻoukou i ko ʻoukou wahi, a ʻo
Kānekoa me kāna wahine ma ʻaneʻi, i mea e haunaele ʻole ai. ʻO ka hele
aku, hele mai, ʻo ia ko ʻoukou mea e pono ai."

Aloha iho nei ʻo Kānekoa i ka punalua a hānai mai nei i mau ʻuala a
kipaku aku. Akā, ʻo ka ʻohana, alualu lākou i kēlā kanaka, a nou aku iā ia
i ka pōhaku. Holo kēlā kanaka no Kona a i laila ʻo ia i make ai. ʻAi iho nei
ka ʻohana a māʻona, hoʻi i Kaʻū.

A ʻī aku nei ʻo Makanikeoe i ke aikāne, "Ua lawa kēia ana no ʻolua – a
ʻo au hoʻi, e hele wau i kuʻu huakaʻi o ke aloha." Honi iho nei ʻo ia iā
lāua, a hele aku nei. A i kona alanui, ʻike iho nei ʻo ia i kekahi wahine
ʻōpio, ua pepehi ʻia e ke kāne a haʻi ka wāwae, a haʻalele. Piha iho nei ʻo
Makanikeoe me ke aloha. Hoʻihoʻi aku nei ʻo ia i kēia ʻōpio i ke ana o
Kānekoa, a ʻī aku nei ʻo ia, "Ke hoʻihoʻi mai nei au i ka mea pilikia iā
ʻolua, a e hana maikaʻi ʻolua iā ia; e aloha mai ʻolua iā ia e like me koʻu
aloha ʻana aku iā ʻolua." A me kēia mau huaʻōlelo, ua hele ʻo Makanikeoe
no kāna huakaʻi o ke aloha.

Inā ua ʻike ka poʻe kahiko o Kaʻū i ka hakakā ʻana ma waena o kekahi

ʻohana, ua ʻōlelo mai lākou, "Ua haʻalele ʻo Makanikeoe i kona hale." A hiki mai ka maluhia i loko o ia hale, ua ʻī mai lākou, "Ua hoʻi mai ʻo Makanikeoe!"

The English-language version of this story, *Makanikeoe, the God of Love,* appears on page 27.

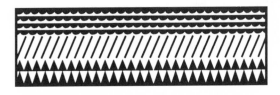

HINAIKEAHI A ME HINAIKAWAI

No Hilo, Hawaiʻi, ʻo Hinaikeahi a me Hinaikawai, a he mau wāhine kupua lāua. ʻO Hinaikeahi ke kaikuaʻana, a ʻo Hinaikawai nō kona muli. I ke kaikuaʻana ka mana e hana i nā mea kūpaianaha me ke ahi, a i ke kaikaina hoʻi me ka wai. Ua māhele ʻia ko lāua mau ʻāina a me ko lāua mau kānaka e ko lāua makuahine, e Hina.

I ka hiki ʻana mai o kekahi wī weliweli ma luna o ka ʻāina, ua nui ka uē o kānaka i ka pōloli. Ua nui nō hoʻi nā keiki liʻiliʻi i make i ka nele o ka makuahine i ka waiū.

Nānā mai nei ʻo Hinaikeahi i kona poʻe kānaka, a ua hū aʻe nei ke aloha iā lākou, no laila ʻo ia i hea mai ai iā lākou e ʻākoakoa aku i kona alo. Kauoha aku nei ʻo ia i nā kāne e ahonui a e hele i ke kuahiwi i ka lapulapu wahie, a i ka muliwai i pōhaku imu. A i ke āhua ʻana o kēia mau mea, e hana i imu ʻenaʻena nui. Kāhāhā ka naʻau o kānaka i ke kauoha ʻia i imu, ʻoiai ʻaʻohe mea ʻai e hoʻomoʻa aku ai. No ke aloha nō i ke aliʻi, hana kunukunu ʻole nō.

I ka mākaukau ʻana o ka imu, hele kaʻapuni aʻe nei ʻo Hinaikeahi, ʻōlelo iho nei, "Ma aneʻi ka ʻuala, ke kalo, ka uhi, ʻīlio, puaʻa, iʻa, hāpuʻu, a me ka moa!" Pau nō kāna ʻōlelo ʻana, hoʻi aku nei ʻo ia i waena o ka imu, a hea maila i kānaka e uhi iā ia i ka lepo.

Uē aʻe nei kānaka, "ʻAʻole! ʻAʻole!" ʻŌlelo mai nei ʻo Hinaikeahi, "E oʻu mau kānaka, mai uē ʻoukou! E uhi mai i ka lepo ma luna oʻu, a e hele aʻe au i nā kūpuna akua o kākou i ola no kākou. E nānā ʻoukou i ke kolu o ka lā, a ʻike ʻoukou i ke ao e kau pono ana ma luna o ka imu nei. I kū he wahine me ke ʻano ʻoliʻoli ke nānā aku, huʻe ʻia ka imu. E uhi mai iaʻu!"

Me ka hopohopo nō i kanu aku ai nā kānaka i ke aliʻi aloha o lākou. I ke kolu o ka lā ua ʻike ʻia he ao, kohu kino wahine, ma luna pono o ka imu, ʻo ko lākou huʻe nō ia i ka imu. ʻAʻohe i loaʻa aku ʻo Hinaikeahi e moe mai ana, akā ʻo nā mea ʻai wale nō āna i helu ai: ʻo ka uhi, ke kalo, ka iʻa, a pēlā wale aku.

Pau nō kā lākou wehewehe ʻana, ʻike ʻia ʻo Hinaikeahi e hoʻi mai ana mai kahakai mai, ua ʻohuʻohu i ka lei limu kala. Me ka ʻāwīwī loa i kuʻi ʻia ai ka ʻai, a noho lākou a pau e pāʻina. Iā lākou e ʻai ana, haʻi mai ʻo Hinaikeahi i kona hele ʻana i nā kūpuna ahi e aloha mai iā lākou. A i ka piha ʻana o kāna imu i ka ʻai, ua hele ʻo ia i ka ʻauʻau kai me Hinaʻōpūhalakoʻa.

E like nō me ke ʻano maʻa mau o kānaka, ʻo ka walaʻau, ua ʻohiʻohi aku nei ko Hinaikeahi mau kānaka i ko Hinaikawai i ka ʻono maoli o nā mea ʻai a ka haku o lākou i hoʻolako ai. Hoʻi aku nei ko Hinaikawai mau kānaka, a uē aku nei i ke aliʻi o lākou, me ka hōʻike pū aku nō hoʻi i nā mea a pau a lākou i lohe mai ai mai nā kānaka o Hinaikeahi mai.

Komo iho nei ka manaʻo lili i loko o Hinaikawai. Kauoha aku nei ʻo ia i nā kānaka e hana i imu nui, a i ka mākaukau ʻana, ua hoʻohālike ʻo ia me kā kona kaikuaʻana i ka helu papa i nā mea ʻai; a pau ia, hea aku nei i nā kānaka e uhi iā ia i ka lepo.

I ke kolu o ka lā, he lā ʻūmāmalu ia; ua ʻike ʻia he ao uliuli, me he wahine lā, e kau pono ana ma luna o ka imu. Me ka ʻeleu loa i huʻe ai nā kānaka i ka imu. Auē! ʻAʻohe ʻai i loaʻa aku, akā ʻo ke kino pāpaʻa wale nō o Hinaikawai!

I ka hāmama ʻana o ka imu, ua hoʻoheleleʻi ka ua, a ua ʻōlelo ʻia, ʻo nā waimaka ia mai ka lani mai no Hinaikawai. Inā ua kiʻi nō ʻo Hinaikawai i kona māhele, he wai, inā nō ia i ola. ʻAʻole naʻe, piʻi koke ka lili, a lele kāmoko i ka mana o ke kaikuaʻana. ʻO ka hopena ia o ka hoʻokiʻekiʻe. ʻIke aʻe nei nā kānaka, ʻaʻohe o lākou haku, ʻaʻohe mea ʻai, ʻo ka hoʻi nō ia o lākou a pau me Hinaikeahi.

The English-language version of this story, *Woman of the Fire and Woman of the Water*, appears on page 30.

KA U'I KEAMALU

No Paliuli 'o Keamalu, no kēlā 'āina kamaha'o i noho 'ia e Lā'iekawai. E like nō me ka hānai punahele 'ia 'ana o Lā'iekawai, pēlā nō ko Keamalu hānai punahele 'ia 'ana. Na nā manu i kia'i iā ia, a i hānai iā ia i nā hua lama, pi'oi, māmaki a me ka wai o ka lehua. 'A'ohe ona 'ai i nā mea 'ē a'e, 'o nā mea wale nō a nā manu i hānai mai ai iā ia.

He pūnāwai ko ke kuahiwi o 'Ōla'a i kapa 'ia ka "pūnāwai o Keamalu," a i laila i hele ai 'o Keamalu e 'au'au. Iā ia e noho ana ma kapa o ka pūnāwai i kekahi lā, ua 'ō'ili maila kekahi kanaka 'ōpio a i kona 'ike 'ana iā Keamalu, 'o kona koi akula nō ia i wahine nāna. Ua hō'ole mai 'o Keamalu, 'a'ohe ona makemake i kāne 'o ia nāna, a no ka pa'akikī loa o kēia kanaka 'ōpio, ua iho mai nā manu a 'o ka lilo nō ia o ua kaikamahine nei i luna o ko lākou mau 'ēheu.

Ua ho'i akula ke kanaka 'ōpio i Puna me kāna ipo aloha, me Kalehua'ula. 'Oiai kona kino i Puna me kēlā wahine u'i, aia nō na'e kona no'ono'o i ka uka o 'Ōla'a. A no ka loa'a 'ole iā ia o ka maha ma ka na'au, ua 'imi hele 'ia e ia ka nahele o 'Ōla'a i nā manawa a pau. A i ka loa'a 'ole 'ana o Keamalu iā ia, ua ho'i akula 'o ia me Kalehua'ula. Ua noho mālie nō 'o Keamalu i ka hale no kekahi manawa lō'ihi no kona maka'u o 'ike hou 'ia mai 'o ia e ke kanaka 'ōpio.

Ua lohe nā mākua o Kalehua'ula i ka 'imi o kēia 'ōpio iā Keamalu a nīnau mai nei me ke 'ano ho'onāukiuki, "He u'i anei kēlā wahine āu e 'imi nei?" "'Ae, he u'i maoli," i pane mai ai ka 'ōpio. "'O kā māua nō ka u'i. No hea ia pālau'eka o kuahiwi i loa'a mai ai kā māua?" He mea 'oia'i'o nō, he u'i 'o Kalehua'ula, koe na'e ke kūkona o nā maka.

Ua noho 'o Keamalu a mana'o no ka lō'ihi loa o kona pe'e 'ana ua poina kēlā kanaka 'ōpio iā ia, a no laila, ua hele hou mai nō ia i ka pūnāwai 'au'au ona. Iā ia nō a hiki iho, 'o ka pa'a nō ia i ka pūliki 'ia, a i hemo wale nō 'o ia i ke kiko 'ia 'ana o ka helehelena a me nā lima o ke kanaka 'ōpio e ka 'io a lilo hou 'o Keamalu i nā manu.

Ua lohe nā kahu hānai kupua o Keamalu i ka 'ōlelo kīkoi a nā mākua o Kalehua'ula a no laila, ua ho'oholo lākou e ho'okūkū i ka u'i o kā lākou me ka u'i o Puna. Ua ho'ouna 'ia ke kanaka e hō'ike i ko lākou nei mana'o i nā mākua o Kalehua'ula. I ko lāua lohe 'ana, ua 'ae mai lāua me ke kānalua 'ole, no ka mea, ua kaulana ka u'i o kā lāua kaikamahine a puni 'o Puna.

'A'ohe lāua i 'ike he hānai 'o Keamalu na nā kupua o Paliuli. A eia ka mea mua i ho'oholo 'ia, e 'ako 'o Keamalu i kāna pua a ho'okomo i loko o kekahi 'umeke nui, a 'o Kalehua'ula i kāna pua a ho'okomo i loko o kāna 'umeke, a 'o ka 'umeke e pōhai 'ia ana e nā manu lā, 'o kā ka u'i ia.

I ka hiki 'ana mai o ka lā ho'okūkū, ua piha kā Kalehua'ula 'umeke i ka hīnano a me ka lehua 'ula, a 'o kā Keamalu i ka maile a me ka lehua kea. Ua pōhai 'ia ka 'umeke a Keamalu e ka 'i'iwi a 'o kā Kalehua'ula ho'i, ho'okahi nō wahi nalo keleawe i lele mai a kau i luna o kāna mau pua. Ua nui ka ho'ohalahala o nā mākua o Kalehua'ula i kēia a koi aku nei e ho'okūkū a'e i nā kaikamāhine. 'O ka makemake nō ia o nā kupua a ua 'ae lākou.

I kahi lā mai, ua kono 'ia nā po'e a pau e hele mai nei e nānā i kēia ho'okūkū nui. I ka hō'ea 'ana mai o Kalehua'ula, ua nui ka mahalo 'ia o kona u'i e nā kānaka, akā, i ka lawe 'ia 'ana mai o Keamalu e kona mau kahu hānai, ua 'ike 'ia a'ela ua 'oi kona u'i ma mua o nā u'i 'ē a'e a lākou i 'ike ai.

Ua ho'ōho a'ela lākou i ka u'i o kēia kaikamahine a ua 'ā'ume'ume nā kānaka no kahi a lākou e 'ike pono aku ai i kēia nani kamaha'o. Ua hoka loa nā mākua o Kalehua'ula a ho'i me ka hilahila i kā lāua mea i kaena makehewa ai. Ua 'ae 'ia ka noi a kēlā kanaka 'ōpio o Puna a ua lilo 'o Keamalu i wahine ho'āo nāna a ua maika'i ko lāua noho 'ana i ka uka o Paliuli.

'O ka pūnāwai o Keamalu, ua nalowale, a he kāka'ikahi loa ka po'e i hō'ike 'ia kēlā pūnāwai.

The English-language version of this story, *The Beautiful Keamalu,* appears on page 32.

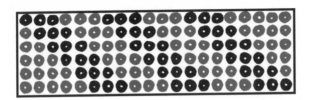

NĀPUAOPĀʻULA

He kaikamahine uʻi loa ʻo Nāpuaopāʻula no Pāʻula, Kaʻū, Hawaiʻi. Ua nui loa ka poʻe i mahalo i ka uʻi o kēia kaikamahine a ua lilo nō hoʻi ʻo ia i mea nui na kona ʻohana. Ma kahi kokoke i ko lākou hale he ʻohana i piha i ka lili iā Nāpuaopāʻula, no ka mea, ua kaulana ʻo ia i ka uʻi, a ʻo kā lākou i ka pupuka.

Aia ma waena o Pāʻula Kai a me Kahaoa kahi i noho ai kekahi ʻaumakua manō o kēia poʻe lili. I nā lā a pau ua hele lākou me ka ʻawa, ka maiʻa me nā mea ʻai maikaʻi ʻē aʻe e hānai i ka manō. ʻO ka mea mua e ninini ʻia ai i lalo i ka lua manō, ʻo ka ʻawa, a ke piʻi mai ke poʻo o ua manō nei, ua hānai ʻia i nā mea ʻai a lākou i lawe mai ai. No ko lākou lili loa iā Nāpuaopāʻula ua kauoha aku nei i ka manō e kinai i kona ola.

I ka hoʻi ʻana mai o Nāpuaopāʻula me nā mākua mai ka mahi ʻai mai a kokoke i kahakai, ua ʻike lākou i ke ōpū nalu i like loa me ka moa uakea i ka piʻi ʻana mai a popoʻi ma luna o Nāpuaopāʻula. He leo uē kā nā mākua i lohe ai a ʻike akula lāua i ka ʻai hoʻomāinoino ʻia o kā lāua kaikamahine e ka manō. Ua huki hele ʻia mai Kahaoa a Kawainui, a mai Kawainui a Kahaoa. Ua uē mai ʻo Nāpuaopāʻula i nā mākua, "E oʻu mau mākua ē, ʻaʻole au e ola ana. Aloha kākou."

No ka minamina loa o nā mākua i ke kaikamahine, ua hele lāua e nīnau i ke kahuna i ke kumu i pōʻino ai ka lei aloha a lāua. Mea mai ke kahuna iā lāua, ua pōʻino i ka ʻaumakua manō o ka poʻe e noho kokoke ala nō ma ko lākou wahi, a inā he aloha keiki ko lāua, e kiʻi i puaʻa hiwa, moa uakea, ʻawa hiwa a lawe mai i mua ona. Ua hoʻokō ʻia kēia mau kauoha a pau.

ʻAʻole i lōʻihi ma hope iho, ua hāpai ka makuahine o Nāpuaopāʻula a hānau mai he kaikamahine. Ua hea ʻia nō kona inoa ʻo Nāpuaopāʻula no kona kaikuaʻana. ʻO ke ʻano nō a pau o ke kaikuaʻana i luna o kēia kaikamahine.

A no kēlā poʻe loko ʻino hoʻi, ua loaʻa lākou i ka maʻi pehu a make. Ua loaʻa mua ka makua kāne i ka maʻi pehu a make, a pehu mai ana ka wahine a make nō. Pēlā i hana ʻia ai a pau loa kēlā ʻohana i ka make, ʻaʻole hoʻokahi i koe.

A no Nāpuaopāʻula ʻōpio a me nā mākua, ua kū lākou a hele loa mai kēlā wahi aku. ʻAʻohe poʻe i hānai hou i kēlā manō ʻino, a ua hoʻomaopopo ʻole ʻia ʻo ia ma nā ʻano a pau. No kēia kumu lā i makaʻu loa ʻia ai kēlā lua manō, no ka ike ʻia he manō ʻino ko loko, he ʻai kanaka.

The English-language version of this story, *Blossoms of Pāʻula*, appears on page 42.

KA MOʻOLELO O ʻIOLE ME PUEO

ʻO Pueo a me ʻIole, he mau kupua lāua no Kohala. ʻO Pueo, he kanaka mahi ʻai ʻo ia, a e hana ana ʻo ia i nā pō a pau, a i ka piʻi ʻana mai o ka lā, hoʻomaha ʻo ia, no ka mea, ʻaʻole hiki i kona mau maka ke ʻike i ka lā. ʻO ʻIole hoʻi, he kanaka palaualelo ʻo ia, a e kaukaʻi ana ʻo ia i kona naʻauao ʻaihue. E hele mau ana ʻo ia e ʻaihue i ka ʻuala a Pueo. A e makaʻala mau ana ʻo Pueo e poʻi i ka ʻIole.

ʻIke ʻo ʻIole e hākilo ana ʻo Pueo i kona hele ʻana i ka māla ʻuala, no laila, ʻeli ʻo ia i lua ma lalo o ka honua a hiki i ua māla ʻuala nei, a ʻai ʻo ia a pau kona makemake i ka hua. Manaʻo ʻo Pueo, ua hele ʻo ʻIole, no ka ʻike hou ʻole ʻia e ʻaihue ana, no laila hoʻonanea ʻo ia. Hoʻokahi pō, hele aku nei ʻo ia e huhuki i ʻuala nāna, a ʻike ihola ʻo ia, ua pau ka nui o nā ʻuala, a e koe kumukumu ana nō kahi.

Piʻi ihola kona inaina, a ʻimi akula ʻo ia i uku pānaʻi nāna. No laila, hākilo akula ʻo ia i ke kahu kanaka o ʻIole e hele ana e ukuhi wai i loko o kāna hue wai no ʻIole. I ka piha ʻana o ka hue wai, lele ihola ʻo ia i lalo, a kiko aku nei a puka ka hue wai. Lālau aʻe nei ke kanaka i ka paukū lāʻau a uhau aku nei iā Pueo. ʻO ka haki nō ia o kahi wāwae o Pueo.

Hea aku nei ʻo ia iā ʻIo, ke kupua ikaika i waena o lākou, "E ʻIo ē! E ʻIo ē! Ua ʻeha au i ke kanaka!" "Na wai ka hewa?" i nīnau mai ai ʻo ʻIo. "Naʻu nō!" wahi a Pueo. "I aha ʻia e ʻoe?" "I kiko ʻia e aʻu ka hue wai a ʻIole." "Kā! Ua hewa ʻoe," i pane mai ai ʻo ʻIo. "Pehea nō lā ʻoe i hana naʻaupō ai?" Uē aʻela ʻo Pueo a hōʻike maila i kona pōloli—no ka pau o ka ʻuala i ka ʻaihue ʻia. Nānā maila ʻo ʻIo i ke kanaka, a ʻike maila ua ʻoi ka ikaika o ke kanaka ma mua ona, e hiki ʻole ai nō iā ia ke kōkua mai iā Pueo.

Noho ʻo Pueo a ola ka wāwae ona, ʻimi aku nei ʻo ia i wahi no ʻIole e pōʻino ai. Hele aku nei ʻo ia i waena o nā poʻe mākaukau i ka pana ʻiole; ʻaʻole naʻe i loaʻa kekahi kanaka i hiki ke pepehi i ke kupu ʻino. Lohe iho nei ʻo Pueo i kekahi kupua pana ʻiole ma Oʻahu, ʻo Pīkoi, ke keiki a ʻAlalā. No laila, hele mai nei ʻo ia e hoʻāikāne, a hōʻike mai nei no kēlā ʻiole ʻaihue.

ʻO ko Pīkoi leʻaleʻa ia ʻo ka pepehi ʻiole, no laila holo aku nei lāua no Hilo. Piʻi aku nei ʻo Pīkoi i luna o Kaʻuiki, a nānā aku nei i Kohala. ʻIke aku nei ʻo ia iā ʻIole, no laila pana aku nei ʻo ia i kāna pua. E noho nanea ana nō ʻo ʻIole, a kū ʻo ia iā Pīkoi, a make loa. ʻO kona wahi i make ai, ua kapa ʻia ʻo ʻIole a hiki i kēia lā. Ma laila e kū nei ka hale pule Kalawina ʻo ʻIole.

The English-language version of this story, *ʻIole the Rat and Pueo the Owl*, appears on page 51.

Naupaka

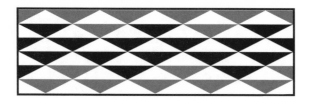

'O PUHI ME LOLI

He mau kupua 'o Puhi me Loli mai ka 'āina 'ē mai a noho i Kona. I ka lā he puhi kekahi a he loli kekahi, a i ka pō he mau kānaka u'i lāua. I kekahi pō mahina ua iho mai kekahi mau kamali'i wahine e 'au'au kai a e lawai'a nō ho'i kekahi. Iā lāua nei e nanea ana i ka lawai'a, ua 'ike 'ia maila lāua e Puhi a me Loli. Ua ho'okokoke mai lāua ma kahi o nā kaika-māhine e noho ana. Ua pū'iwa nā kaikamāhine i ka 'ike 'ana i kēia mau kānaka u'i ma ko lāua 'ao'ao. A i ka 'ike 'ana o kēia mau kānaka i ka u'i o kēia mau kaikamāhine, 'o ko lāua ho'omaka maila nō ia i ke kama'ilio me ka leo ho'ohenoheno.

'O ka ho'oha'i koke ihola nō ia o kēia mau kaikamāhine. I ka ho'i 'ana o nā kaikamāhine i kauhale o lākou, 'a'ole loa lāua i ho'opuka aku i kekahi mau hua'ōlelo e pili ana i kēia mau malihini, no ko lāua 'ike i ka 'ōlelo pa'a a ko lāua makua, 'a'ohe ona makemake i kāne malihini a kupua paha na lāua.

He mau malama ma hope iho, ua ho'ohuoi ka makua kāne i ka 'ono 'ole mai o nā kaikamāhine i ka 'ai, i ke ake mau i ka napo'o koke aku o ka lā a me ka hele mau i kahakai a ho'i mai me ka nele. No laila, i kekahi pō, ua hahai aku 'o ia ma hope o lāua me ko lāua 'ike 'ole mai. Ua 'ike aku nei 'o ia i ka ho'i 'ana o nā kaikamāhine ma ka waha o kekahi ana 'u'uku e noho ai, a i mea e hiki ai iā ia ke 'ike pono i kā lāua mea e hana ai, ua kokolo aku nei 'o ia ma hope o kekahi mau pōhaku nunui ma ka 'ao'ao o kāheka.

'A'ole nō 'o ia i lō'ihi ma laila, 'ike aku nei 'o ia i kekahi puhi a me ka loli e pi'i mai ana a kū ā kānaka. 'A'ole na'e 'o ia i 'ike 'ia mai e lāua. Iā ia e hākilo ana, 'ike aku nei 'o ia i ka pi'i 'ana a nonoho me kāna mau kaika-māhine. Ma laila nō 'o ia, kahi i hākilo ai, a ho'i mai nei ua mau kānaka nei a i ua kāheka nei nō, a lilo a'e nei kekahi i puhi a 'o kekahi i loli, a ho'i aku nei i loko o ke kai. 'Āwīwī aku nei 'o ia a komo i ka hale ma mua o ka hō'ea 'ana a'e o nā kaikamāhine. 'Ano kāhāhā lāua i ka huhū 'ole o ka

127

makua kāne e like me ka mea maʻa mau, i ko lāua hele wale nō i kahakai e pāʻani ai a hoʻi ukana ʻole mai i ka hale.

I kekahi pō mai, ma hope o ka iho ʻana o nā kaikamāhine i kahakai, ua hele malū aʻela ʻo ia i kahakai, a i kona ʻike ʻana iā Puhi a me Loli e hoʻo-ipoipo ana me kāna mau kaikamāhine, ua hoʻomoe aʻela ʻo ia i kāna ʻupena ma kahi āna i ʻike ai i nā malihini e hoʻi ana. I ka hoʻi ʻana mai o Puhi a me Loli, ua hihia lāua i ka ʻupena a paʻa loa. Ua huki ʻia lāua i uka a noke ʻia i ke kīpōpō me ka pōhaku a make loa. I kēlā pō, ua hoʻihoʻi ʻia lāua i kauhale a kālua ʻia a moʻa.

I ke ala ʻana mai o nā kaikamāhine, ʻī aku nei ka makua kāne,

"He iʻa anei kā ʻolua i ka pō nei?"

"ʻAʻohe iʻa, he kai koʻo," wahi a lāua.

"ʻAe, he mea ʻoiaʻiʻo kēnā. Ua hele au i ka lawaiʻa i ka pō nei a ʻo kahi mea nō i paʻa, he puhi a he loli. Ua moʻa aʻe nei iaʻu, a e hele mai ʻolua e ʻai."

"ʻAʻole kā ʻoe e ʻai ana me māua?"

"ʻAʻole, ua ʻai mua nō au a māʻona." ʻO ko lāua noho nō ia e ʻai a māʻona.

I ka māʻona ʻana, ʻī mai nei ka makua kāne iā lāua, "ʻĀ ʻo ia! ʻAi ihola nō ʻolua i ke kino iʻa o nā kāne a ʻolua!" Ua kū ā maʻi kēia mau kaika-māhine i ka lohe ʻana i kēia, a holo aku nei i waho e luaʻi ai. Iā lāua e luaʻi nei, ua kū maila ka makua kāne me ka paukū lāʻau nui.

Luaʻi mai nei kekahi he loli liʻiliʻi, a ʻo kekahi he puhi liʻiliʻi; ua ola a e ʻoni ana e hoʻi hou i kahakai. Pepehi ʻia ka puhi a me ka loli e ka makua kāne o nā kaikamāhine me ka paukū lāʻau a make a puhi ʻia i ke ahi a lehu. ʻO ka lehu, ua lawe ʻia e kanu i ka ʻāina wai ʻole, i ʻole ai e ola hou mai. No nā kaikamāhine hoʻi, ua noho nō lāua a loaʻa nā kāne kūpono i kū i ka makemake o ka makua kāne.

The English-language version of this story, *The Eel and the Sea Cucumber,* appears on page 53.

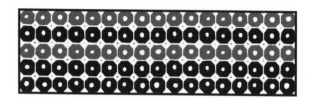

PEKEKUE

No Moloka'i 'o Mānoanoa. Mai kona wā 'u'uku loa mai kona makemake 'ana i ka 'ai he'e. Ua kaulana 'o ia i ka puni he'e. I nā lā a pau e komo mai ai nā 'au wa'a lawai'a, ua hele 'o ia i ka lae kahakai i he'e nāna. Inā nō e ho'ounauna 'ia mai, hana nō 'o ia, a 'o kona uku he he'e. Ke 'u'uku loa nā he'e e loa'a i nā lawai'a, ua 'oli'oli nō 'o ia inā e loa'a ka 'awe'awe ho'okahi.

I kekahi lā ua loa'a mai iā ia he he'e nui. Ho'iho'i 'ia e ia, a kaula'i 'ia kekahi mau 'awe'awe i luna o ka lālā lā'au, a 'o ke koena ua pokepoke 'ia, me ka mana'o, aia a pau kāna hana, ho'i mai e 'ai. Ua hele akula 'o ia ma kahi 'ao'ao o kona hale e hana ai i kekahi mau hana li'ili'i āna.

Ua nanea loa 'o Mānoanoa i ka hana, a pū'iwa a'e nei i ka lohe 'ana i kekahi leo e 'ōlelo ana, "Pekekue!" Nānā aku nei 'o ia ma 'ō a ma 'ane'i, 'a'ohe mea āna i 'ike aku ai. I kona lohe hou 'ana i kēlā leo e hea ana, "E Pekekue!" ua 'alawa aku nei 'o ia i luna o kona hale, a 'ike aku nei 'o ia i ka he'e e 'eu mai ana. Ua ho'i hou nā 'awe'awe a hui hou me ka pū!

Me ka maka'u nui i nānā aku ai 'o Mānoanoa. I ke kokoke loa 'ana mai, 'ōlelo a'e nei ka he'e, "E Pekekue, e 'ai 'ia nā 'awe'awe a koe nō ka pū." I ia manawa nō, lele a'e nei ka he'e a kuhō aku nei i loko o ka pūnāwai, kokoke nō i kahi a Mānoanoa e noho ana, a nalowale.

Mai kēlā lā mai, ua kau loa ka weli o Mānoanoa i ka he'e. 'A'ole loa 'o ia i hele hou i kahakai e kakali ai i nā 'au wa'a e ho'i mai ana, i he'e. I ka hānau 'ana o kāna mo'opuna, ua hea 'ia 'o Pekekue, ka inoa a ka he'e i kāhea ai iā ia.

The English-language version of this story, *Pekekue*, appears on page 57.

He mo'olelo kēia e hō'ike ana i ke kumu i mālama loa 'ia ai ka ipu 'awa-'awa e kekahi po'e o Ka'ū, Hawai'i. Ua 'ōlelo 'ia, he ali'i wahine ko Ka'ū i aloha nui 'ia e kona po'e kānaka. I ka hāpai 'ana o ua ali'i nei, ua hiki mai ka ma'i ma luna ona, a i ke kokoke 'ana aku i ka wā e hānau ai, ua make ihola ke ali'i wahine. Ua lawe 'ia kona kino i loko o ke ana. Ua 'oloka'a 'ia ka pōhaku nui a pa'a ka waha o ka lua.

I ka hiki 'ana mai o ka lā e hānau ai 'o ke keiki, ua 'ō'ili mai ka mu'o mai ka piko mai o ke ali'i make, a ulu a puka ma kekahi hakahaka 'u'uku ma ka 'ao'ao o ka pani o ka lua, a kolo aku nei no kahi mamao loa aku. I kekahi kakahiaka ua 'ike akula ke ali'i o ka hiku o nā ahupua'a i kolo 'ia e ka ipu 'awa'awa i ka ulu maika'i mai ma hope aku o kona hale.

Ua mālama 'ia e ia a hiki i ka pua 'ana a hua. I ke o'o 'ana iho, ua hele mau 'o ia i nā lā a pau e kīkēkē, e 'iniki, e nānā ai inā i o'o maika'i e kaha-kaha 'ia ai. 'A'ole i 'ike kēia ali'i he ipu 'awa'awa kanaka kēia.

Ua ho'i ka 'uhane o kēia ipu 'awa'awa i luna o kekahi haka a hō'ike aku nei i kona 'iniki 'ia, a ua nui ka 'eha. Ki'i 'ia ke kahuna o kēlā wahi a ua hō'ike 'ia iā ia e ka ipu 'awa'awa nā mea i hāhā 'ia ma luna o kona kino, me ke kauoha pū aku iā ia e 'imi a loa'a 'o ia a ho'iho'i mai. Ua iho ke kahuna a ka lua pao, a ma laila 'o ia i ho'okolo ai ma ke kā o ka ipu 'awa'awa, a hiki i ka hiku o nā ahupua'a.

I ka 'ike 'ana o ke ali'i iā ia ma kahi o ka ipu 'awa'awa, nīnau maila 'o ia no ke aha 'o ia nei i hiki aku ai. Hō'ike aku nei ua kahuna nei i ka hō'ike a kona haku iā ia. Ua piha ke ali'i i ka minamina i kona nānā 'ana iho i ka maika'i o ka ipu 'awa'awa, a hō'ole aku nei i ka mana'o o ke kahuna.

Ua lilo ihola kēia i kumu no lāua e ho'opa'apa'a ai a hiki i ka 'ōlelo 'ana aku o ke kahuna e hele lāua a 'ike pono 'o wai ka i kuleana 'i'o i ua ipu 'awa'awa lā; 'o ke kumu mai, no ka hilina'i 'ole o ke ali'i he kanaka nō kēia ipu 'awa'awa. I ka 'ae 'ana o ke ali'i, ua hele lāua e 'ike i kahi i kupu a'e ai 'o ua ipu 'awa'awa lā. Ua hele lāua ma ka 'ao'ao o ke kā a hiki i ka lua pao, a komo aku nei i loko. Ua 'ike like aku nei nō lāua i kahi i ulu mai ai 'o ka ipu 'awa'awa, mai ka 'ōpū mai o ke ali'i make.

Ua ho'iho'i 'ia mai ka ipu 'awa'awa e ke kahuna a mālama 'ia me ka punahele loa a hiki i ka make 'ana o ua kahuna nei. Ma hope mai o ia manawa, 'a'ole i maopopo he aha lā ka mea i hana 'ia no kēlā ipu 'awa'awa.

No ka 'ohana o kēlā wahine ali'i i make, ua lilo loa ka ipu 'awa'awa i mea nui iā lākou. Ke nahā kā lākou ipu 'awa'awa, ua kanu 'ia me ka mai-ka'i, a i 'ole, ua puhi 'ia i ke ahi i 'ole e kāpulu 'ia. Ke nīnau 'ia aku ke kumu o lākou i kiloi wale 'ole ai i nā 'āpa'apana o kā lākou ipu 'awa'awa, ho'okahi nō pane e loa'a mai, "No ka hiku o nā ahupua'a."

The English-language version of this story, *The Seventh District*, appears on page 62.

NĀ ALI'I HO'OLUHI O KA'Ū

Ua kapa 'ia kēlā 'āina ma waena o Kona a me Puna 'o Ka'ū, he 'āina mākaha. He 'ekolu ali'i ho'oluhi o ia wahi i ka wā kahiko, a penei ko lākou mau mo'olelo.

HALA'EA

He ali'i 'ānunu i'a 'o Hala'ea. I kēlā lā a me kēia lā e hele ana 'o ia e nānā i nā 'au wa'a lawai'a a kānaka, a lawe a'ela i nā i'a a pau nāna a me kona 'ōhua. Ua 'ai 'uha'uha lākou i ka i'a, he ho'omāunauna maoli i kahi wā. 'O nā kānaka ho'i, 'o ka lawai'a wale iho nō, 'a'ohe kahi i'a e ho'iho'i aku ai i ka 'ohana. Hala nō ka lā i ka lau nahele o ka 'āina.

Oi hana mau ihola nō ia o ke ali'i penei, a uluhua kānaka, a 'imi i wahi no lākou e maha ai i kā Hala'ea mau hana ho'oluhi. 'A'ohe wā a lākou i hele ai i ka moana a ho'i mai i nele ai nō ho'i i ka leo o ka haku o lākou i ka hea mai, "Na'u ka i'a! Mai, na'u kēnā i'a!"

I ka wā kau ʻahi, ua kuahaua ʻia i nā poʻo lawaiʻa e hele pū me ke aliʻi i ka lawaiʻa ʻahi. Hoʻākoakoa nā poʻo lawaiʻa i ko lākou mau waʻa, nā ʻupena, maunu, a pēlā wale aku, a kūkākūkā iho nei lākou e hāʻawi i kā lākou iʻa a pau loa i ke aliʻi, a hoʻi pololei i ka ʻāina me ka nānā ʻole aku i hope. I ka hiki ʻana mai o ka lā i koho ʻia no ka lawaiʻa ʻana, ua ʻākoakoa nā waʻa mai Waiʻahukini a Keauhou.

I ka loaʻa ʻana o ka iʻa a ka waʻa mua, hoʻīli ʻia a pau i luna o ka waʻa o ke aliʻi, a laila hoʻi i uka i kuaone. ʻAʻole i pau ka hea ʻana a ke aliʻi, "Mai, naʻu ka iʻa! Mai, naʻu ka iʻa!" Pēlā i hana ʻia ai e ka lua o ka waʻa, ʻo ke kolu, a ka hā, ka lima, a pēlā wale aku, a piha loa ka waʻa o ke aliʻi i ka iʻa.

ʻIke iho nei ke aliʻi i ke ʻano pihō piholo o ka waʻa i ke kaumaha i ka iʻa, kāhea maila, "Ua lawa ke aliʻi i ka iʻa!"—"ʻAʻole pēlā," wahi a kānaka, "Eia mai ka puni a ke aliʻi!" Hoʻomau nō lākou i ka hoʻoili i ka iʻa, a ka waʻa hope loa nō hoʻi, piholo ka waʻa o ke aliʻi. Nānā aʻe nei ke aliʻi i kōkua nona, ʻaʻohe waʻa kokoke ma laila, ʻaʻohe kanaka nāna e aloha mai—ua pau loa i ka hoʻi!

A make nō ʻo Halaʻea i ke kai, i waena o nā puni a ua aliʻi ʻānunu nei.

KOIHALA

No Kaʻū nō kēia aliʻi hoʻoluhi ʻo Koihala. I kona hele ʻana i Kona, ua hoʻounauna aku nei ʻo ia i kāna kūkini e holo i Kaʻū e ʻōlelo i nā kānaka e hoʻomākaukau i ka ʻai, a hele aʻe i Waiʻahukini e kali ai iā ia. I ka mākaukau ʻana o nā mea ʻai, ua hele nā kānaka i Waiʻahukini.

Iā lākou e nonoho nei, ʻike ʻia ka waʻa a ke aliʻi e holo ana i Kāʻilikiʻi. ʻO ka hāpai nō ia o nā kānaka i nā mea ʻai, a hele i kahi i manaʻo ʻia ai e pae ana ke aliʻi. ʻAʻole naʻe pēlā; iā lākou nei a hiki i Kāʻilikiʻi, ua hoʻi hou ke aliʻi i Kapuʻa!

Hāpai nō kānaka i ka ʻai, a hahai nō ma uka. Iā lākou nei a hiki i Kapuʻa, ʻike ʻia ke aliʻi e holo ana i Kaʻaluʻalu. Hoʻi hou nō kānaka i laila.

Ua hele nā kino a māluhiluhi, no laila hoʻoholo lākou e nānā, a inā e pae koke ʻole ke aliʻi, e ʻai a pau ka ʻai. ʻAʻohe nō i hoʻopae ke aliʻi i kona waʻa, akā, ua noho nō i waho e nānā ai i kānaka. ʻO ka nonoho nō ia o kānaka e ʻai, a pau, hoʻopiha ʻia nā laulau a me nā ʻumeke i ka pōhaku.

ʻIke ke aliʻi i ke ʻano ʻē o kānaka, hoe ʻino ʻo ia i ka waʻa ona, a komo i Kaʻaluʻalu; no kēia kumu i hiki mai ai kēia ʻōlelo noʻeau, "Kau ʻino ʻau waʻa o Kaʻaluʻalu." Piʻi aku nei ʻo ia a kahi a kānaka e nonoho mai ana, hea aku nei, "ʻEa! E ʻai kākou, e ʻai ke aliʻi!" "ʻAe!" i pane mai ai nā kānaka, "Eia kō ʻai me kō iʻa!" ʻO ka hailuku ʻia nō ia o ua aliʻi hoʻoluhi nei, a make loa!

KOHĀIKALANI

He aliʻi hoʻounauna ʻino ʻo Kohāikalani. E ʻimi mau ana ʻo ia i hana kaumaha no nā kānaka. I kona kūkulu ʻana i kona heiau i ka puʻu Kaʻulakalani, ua kauoha ʻia kānaka e kiʻi i ka pōhaku ʻalā i Kāwā, he wahi mamao aku ia. Ua hoʻomanawanui nō lākou i ka ʻauamo ʻana, mai ke kai a ka puʻu a ke kahua o ka heiau.

I ka lawa ʻana o ka pōhaku, ua hōʻea mai he mau kāhuna e nānā i ke ʻano o ke kūkulu ʻana o ka heiau, a i ko lāua ʻike ʻana i nā pōhaku ʻalā o Kāwā, ʻo ko lāua huli mai nō ia i nā kānaka me ka ʻī ʻana, "ʻAuē! He nui nō hoʻi nā pōhaku ma ʻaneʻi, ʻo ko ʻoukou hoʻoluhi ʻia nō kā ia e hele i Kāwā i pōhaku! I paʻa ka heiau o ke aliʻi o ʻoukou, ʻo ko ʻoukou kino nō ka luaahi! I kauoha aʻe nei iā ʻoukou i ʻōhiʻa, ʻōlelo aku nāna nō e kiʻi i kāna, a na ʻoukou e huki i luna nei. A laila hoʻi paha, ola ʻoukou!"

Hoʻolohe nā kānaka i ke aʻo o kēia mau kāhuna. I ka hoʻouna ʻia ʻana e hele ma lalo o ka pali i kumu ʻōhiʻa, pane maila kānaka, "E Kalani ē! Nānā ʻoe a kāu lāʻau i makemake ai, kulaʻi ʻoe, a na mākou e hāpai mai i luna nei." ʻAe nō ke aliʻi. No ka ikaika loa, hoʻokahi nō uhuki ʻana, hemo ke kumu ʻōhiʻa nui!

I ka pau ʻana o nā lālā i ka ʻokiʻoki, ʻōlelo mai nei ke aliʻi e hoʻi ʻo ia i luna e huki ai i ke kaula i hoʻopaʻa ʻia ai ke kumu ʻōhiʻa, a na lākou e pahu aʻe ma lalo. Hōʻole aku nei kānaka, na lākou e huki, a na ke aliʻi e pahu, ʻoiai ua ʻoi kona ikaika i ko lākou. ʻAe nō hoʻi ke aliʻi i kā lākou noi. Huki kānaka i ka ʻōhiʻa a hapalua like o ka pali, hoʻokuʻu lākou i ke kaula. ʻO ke kakaʻa nō ia o ke kumu o ka ʻōhiʻa ma luna o ke aliʻi, a ʻo ka make nō ia o ua aliʻi hoʻoluhi nei!

Ma hope mai o ke au o kēia poʻe aliʻi hoʻoluhi, ua kaulana ʻo Kaʻū i ka mākaha. He makaʻu nā aliʻi i ka ʻōlelo aʻe, "He aliʻi nui mākou!" He ʻāina aliʻi ʻo Kaʻū; na kekahi aliʻi ka hoʻounauna, hoʻokō kekahi; a na kahi ke kauoha, hana kekahi. Pēlā lākou i noho ai, a na kēia au naʻauao i hoʻokāhuli i ia mau mea a pau.

The English-language version of this story, *The Despotic Chiefs of Kaʻū*, appears on page 74.

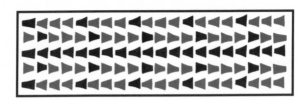

NĀNAELE

He wahine aliʻi ʻo Nānaele, no Kaʻalāiki, Kaʻū, Hawaiʻi. He ʻoluʻolu ʻo ia, he uʻi, a he punahele ma nā ʻano a pau i kona poʻe kānaka. I kekahi lā, ua hele mai kekahi poʻe o Kohala e mākaʻikaʻi ma Kaʻū, a i ko lākou ʻike ʻana iā Nānaele, hoʻohihi aku nei i wahine na kā lākou keiki, na Nāliko. I ka noi ʻia ʻana iā Nānaele, ua ʻae ʻo ia no ka lilo ʻana i wahine no kā lākou keiki, ʻoiai ua ʻōlelo mai lākou he kanaka ʻoluʻolu, he uʻi, he akahai, he hana, a pēlā wale aku.

I ka hoʻi ʻana o kēlā poʻe i Kohala, ua hōʻike akula lākou iā Nāliko i ka nani o Nānaele, me ka noi pū aku nō hoʻi iā ia i kāne na kēlā uʻi nohea o Kaʻū. Hauʻoli aʻe nei ka naʻau o Nāliko i ka wae ʻia ʻana i wahine maikaʻi loa nāna, a ua hāʻawi koke maila i kona ʻae. Mau malama pōkole mai ia manawa mai, ua hoʻāo ʻia kēia mau ʻōpio ma Kaʻalāiki. Ua hiki mai nā hoa aloha, nā makamaka a nā ʻohana i ka ʻahaʻaina nui i hoʻomākaukau ʻia ma laila. Mau lā iho ma hope, ua hoʻi aku ʻo Nānaele me Nāliko i Kohala.

ʻAʻole nō i lōʻihi ko lāua noho ʻana, ua hele hou nō ʻo Nāliko i kāna puni, ʻo ka hula a me nā wāhine ʻōpio o kona one hānau. Haʻalele ʻia ʻo Nānaele i ka hale me ka nele i ka ʻai a me ka iʻa. Hoʻokahi nō āna hana, ʻo ke kakali a aloha ʻia mai e ke kāne, a hoʻihoʻi mai paha i mea e ʻai aʻe ai. ʻAʻole naʻe pēlā. ʻO ke emi mai nō ia o ke kino o Nānaele a koe nā iwi.

I ka hoʻi ʻana mai o ke kāne ʻauana, huli aku nei ʻo Nānaele, a ʻī aku nei,—"E Nāliko ē! Noʻu ke ola hou, ʻaʻole au i ʻike iā ʻoe. He keu kā hoʻi ʻoe a ke aloha ʻole!" "Ē! Ola ʻoe, ola ʻo Milu!" i pane mai ai ʻo Nāliko, a hele hou akula nō i ka ʻimi leʻaleʻa.

I ke kāne nō a hele, kolo aku nei ʻo Nānaele i ka huli mea ʻai. Kolo aku nei a kahi hānai puaʻa a kekahi mau kānaka mahi ʻai, a no ka nāwaliwali loa, hina aku nei a moe. I ka ʻike ʻana mai nei o kekahi kanaka i ka pīʻōʻō o nā puaʻa, hele mai nei e nānā. I kona ʻike ʻana he wahine nāwaliwali loa, ʻauamo aku nei a i kona pupupu hale.

Mālama ʻia ʻo Nānaele e ka wahine a kēlā kanaka a ʻoʻoleʻa iki; haʻi ʻia aku nei ka lono i Kaʻū, ua ʻaneʻane ʻo Nānaele e make. Ua lilo kēia mea hou i mea hoʻokaumaha i nā kānaka o Kaʻalāiki me Kāwā, no laila, ua hele maila lākou e kiʻi i ko lākou haku wahine. I Kahuku kekahi poʻe, i nā Kona kekahi, a i Kohala kekahi. ʻElua kanaka i hiki aku i kahi o Nānaele e noho ana, me ka mānele, a ua ʻauamo akahele ʻia e lāua a hiki i kahi mamao, a ma laila nō hoʻi kekahi poʻe e kali ana iā lākou. Hāpai ʻia aku nei ʻo Nānaele e kekahi mau kānaka hou, ʻoiai ua māluhiluhi nā kānaka mua. Pēlā i hoʻololiloli ʻia ai nā kānaka a hiki i ko lākou hōʻea ʻana i Kaʻalāiki, Kaʻū.

I ka piha ʻana o ka makahiki a ʻoi, ua lohe aku nei ʻo Nāliko ua ola loa ʻo Nānaele, a ua pāpālua aku kona uʻi, a ua nui nō hoʻi nā kāne mai ka uka a ke kai o Kaʻū makemake iā ia i wahine. ʻO ke kū maila nō o ua kāne aloha ʻole nei e kiʻi i kāna wahine e hoʻi hou me ia i Kohala. ʻIke ʻia ʻo ia e kekahi mau kānaka o Nānaele i ka hele aku, ʻo ka holo ʻia nō ia e hōʻike i nā mākua o ka wahine. Hoʻihoʻi ʻia ʻo Nānaele i Kāwā e hūnā ai. Hana ʻia i ʻahaʻaina nui ma Kaʻalāiki no Nāliko. I kona hōʻea ʻana mai, ua hoʻo-kipa maikaʻi ʻia ʻo ia e nā mākua hōnōai, a ua ʻōlelo ʻia mai e lāua, ua hele ʻo Nānaele me kāna haiā wahine i ka ʻauʻau kai, a ahiahi loa hoʻi mai. Hoʻonanea ʻo Nāliko i ka nānā i nā wāhine hula e haʻa ana, a e hula ana i kēia mele,

> Noʻu, no Nānaele
> Na ka wahine a Nāliko.
> Noʻu ke ola aʻe,
> ʻAʻole au i ʻike hou iā ʻoe.

Pane maila kekahi mau wāhine ʻōpio,

> ʻĒ! Ola ʻoe, ola ʻo Milu,
> Kēlā mea i lalo lilo loa!

ʻAʻole i hāʻupu ʻo Nāliko, nona kēia hula e hana ʻia nei. Ua manaʻo nā kānaka e hoʻonanea ʻia ʻo ia a uhi mai ʻo Pō i kona kapa pouli ma luna o ka ʻāina, a laila pepehi, a hūnā iā ia i loko o ka lua pao. Nānā mai nei kekahi ʻelemakule a aloha; hāwanawana malū mai nei, "ʻO kou make kēia! Ma ʻaneʻi nō hoʻi, mai hoʻohākālia o pōʻino. Naʻu ʻoe e alakaʻi a kahi ou e nalo ai. Hoʻi!" Nānā ʻo Nāliko a ka wā e nanea ai ʻo kamaʻāina, ʻo ka holo aku nei nō ia me ka ʻelemakule. Ma lalo lāua o ke ana i hele ai; ʻo ka hele, ʻo ka hoʻomaha, hele a hoʻomaha, a hiki nō hoʻi lāua ma uka o Kapāpala.

Holo lāua ma waena o Hualālai me Mauna Loa, a mai laila aku i ho'i ho'okahi aku ai 'o Nāliko i kona 'āina, a huli ho'i mai ka 'elemakule i Ka'ū o ha'oha'o 'ia 'o ia, a ho'ohuoi 'ia nāna i ho'omahuka iā Nāliko. I ka ho'i 'ana mai o ua 'elemakule nei, ua 'ike 'o ia i kānaka e huli ana iā Nāliko, 'o kona hui aku nei nō ia me lākou. 'Imi 'ia nā wahi a pau mai Kahuku a ka lua o Pele, 'a'ole i loa'a iki.

Pau loa nō ka mana'o 'ana o Nāliko e loa'a hou iā ia 'o Nānaele. Hū maila ke aloha i ka wahine ho'omanawanui, a ho'omana'o a'ela nō ho'i i kāna 'ōlelo, "E ku'u kāne aloha 'ole, no'u ke ola hou, 'a'ole au i 'ike hou iā 'oe!" He 'oia'i'o ia, ua 'ike a'ela nō ia, he make wale nō kona i kānaka o Ka'alāiki. No Nānaele ho'i, ua hau'oli 'o ia i ka ho'i hou i ka poli aloha o kona mau mākua, a e ho'ohau'oli ai ho'i i ka na'au o kona mau kānaka.

Pīpī holo ka'ao.

The English-language version of this story, *The Story of Nānaele*, appears on page 77.

ʻŌhai

KEKAHI MOʻOLELO E PILI ANA NO
KE ALIʻI KAMEHAMEHA I

Ma hope iho o ke kaua ʻana o Kamehameha a me Kalanikūpule i ka lele a ka ʻanae, ua hele akula kekahi o nā koa o Kamehameha i mua o nā ʻaialo, a kaena ihola iā ia iho me ka ʻī ʻana, ʻo ia nō ko Kamehameha kaikaina ponoʻī.

I ka lohe ʻana o ka pūkaua, ukiuki kona naʻau, a ʻī maila ʻo ia, "Kāhāhā! Na wai i ʻōlelo mai iā ʻoe, e ke kanaka piʻikoi, he pili ʻoe iā Kalani? He keu nō, a he hoʻokano!" "ʻAe, he ʻoiaʻiʻo nō," wahi a ua kanaka nei, "ʻo au kona pōkiʻi, a ʻo ia kuʻu hānau mua." I ka lohe ʻana o ka pūkaua i kēia mau ʻōlelo, piha loa ʻo ia i ka inaina. "Hoʻokahi nō pōkiʻi o Kalani, ʻo ia ʻo Keliʻimaikaʻi; ʻaʻole paha ʻo ʻoe, e ka mahaʻoi!"

A ma kēia wahi, pau ko lāua ʻōlelo ʻana. Hele akula ka pūkaua i mua o ke aliʻi, a kamaʻilio aku i nā mea a pau āna i lohe mai ai mai ua kanaka mai. A laila kauoha maila ke aliʻi, "E kiʻi ʻoe i ke kupu ʻino a lawe mai i mua oʻu."

I ka hōʻea ʻana mai o ua kanaka nei, kolo mai ʻo ia i mua o ke aliʻi. Kū maila ke aliʻi, a ʻōlelo maila me ka leo nui,

"Ē! ʻOiaʻiʻo nō anei kēia aʻu i lohe iho nei, ua ʻōlelo ʻoe, e ke kanaka piʻikoi, ʻo wau, ʻo ke aliʻi, kou hānau mua?"

"ʻAe, e Kalani, he ʻoiaʻiʻo nō!"

"A na wai i ʻōlelo iā ʻoe he kaikaina ʻoe noʻu?" wahi a ke aliʻi.

"Nāu nō, e kuʻu haku!"

"Kāhāhā! Ināhea nei wau i ʻōlelo ai iā ʻoe pēlā?"

"I ka hele ʻana o kākou e kaua ma Oʻahu a Kākuhihewa, ua huli mai ʻoe iā mākou, a ʻī mai ʻoe *I mua e nā pōkiʻi, a inu i ka wai ʻawaʻawa!* a i kuʻu lohe ʻana i kēia ʻōlelo maikaʻi a ke aliʻi, ʻo ia koʻu mea e kaena nei he pōkiʻi au nou! A i mua kāua i hele ai a ua inu like i ka wai ʻawaʻawa."

I ka lohe ʻana o ke aliʻi i kēia mau ʻōlelo noʻeau, ʻakaʻaka ihola ia, a kauoha aku i kānaka e hana i ʻahaʻaina no kona pōkiʻi hou!

The English-language version of this story, *A Story of Kamehameha* I, appears on page 81.

139

HE MOʻOLELO E PILI ANA
NO KAMEHAMEHA I

I ka maʻi hope ʻana o Kamehameha, ua ʻiʻini ʻo ia e loaʻa iā ia ka hoʻo-maopopo ʻana i ka lā ona e make ai. Kauoha aku nei ʻo ia i kona mau kāhuna e hele mai i ona lā. I ka nīnau ʻia ʻana aku, "Āhea e make ai ke aliʻi?" Ua hōʻāʻā lākou i ka mea e pane mai ai.

No laila i kauoha aku ai ke aliʻi i kekahi kanaka āna i hilinaʻi nui ai e hele mai. I ka hiki ʻana mai o ua kanaka nei, ʻōlelo maila ke aliʻi iā ia, "E kiʻi ʻoe i puaʻa hiwa, a e hele i Maui, i kuʻu kanaka, iā Pōpolo. Inā ʻoe e pae i ka ʻāina, e hoʻokuʻu aku ʻoe i ka puaʻa, a nāna nō e alakaʻi iā ʻoe a hiki i ka hale. ʻAʻole e nalowale iā ʻoe ʻo Pōpolo; e hele ana nō ka puaʻa a make i kona alo."

Hoʻokō aku nei ua kanaka nei i nā mea a pau i kauoha ʻia iā ia. I ka hiki ʻana i Maui, ua alakaʻi nō ua puaʻa nei iā ia a hiki i kona make ʻana i mua o Pōpolo. Ua loaʻa mua akula nō ka hōʻike iā Pōpolo, he malihini ana kāna mai Hawaiʻi mai, me ka mea hou hoʻokaumaha no ka naʻi aupuni. Hoʻokipa maila ʻo ia i ka malihini, a i ka lohe ʻana i nā manaʻo o ke aliʻi, ua hoʻoholo ʻo ia i kona manaʻo e hele me ka ʻelele i Hawaiʻi.

I kona hiki ʻana aku, ua nīnau maila ke aliʻi, "Āhea au e make ai?" Pane maila kēlā, "Aia a kau ʻo Hoku." Pau aʻela ia, huli mai ke aliʻi i kona ʻohana, a kaukau maila iā lākou, me ka haʻi pū mai nō hoʻi i nā mea āna i makemake ai iā lākou e hana ma hope o kona make ʻana.

I ka pō ʻo Hoku, ʻike maila ʻo Pōpolo i nā hailona i luna o ke ao. Huli aʻela i nā kānaka me ka uē, "ʻO Kalani, ua hala!" I ia pō nō i make ai ʻo Kamehameha I. No kēia kumu i kapa ʻia ai kekahi poʻe aliʻi ʻo Leleiō-hoku, no ka mea, i ka pō ʻo Hoku i lele loa ai ke aho o ka naʻi aupuni.

The English-language version of this story, *Two Stories About Kamehameha I*, appears on page 83. There is no Hawaiian-language version of the second story.

KEAHIʻĀLOA

I ka hānau ʻia ʻana o Keahiʻāloa, ua lawe hānai ʻia ʻo ia e ke kaikuaʻana o kona lūauʻi makuahine. I ka piha ʻana iā ia he ʻehiku makahiki, ua haʻa-lele lāua i ka ʻāina hānau, iā Hawaiʻi, a hoʻi aku nei i Kauaʻi e noho ai.

I ko lāua hiki ʻana i laila, lilo aku nei ka makuahine i ka leʻaleʻa me nā poʻe makaleho o ia ʻāina. ʻO ka pau loa nō ia o kona hoʻomaopopo ʻana i kāna hānai. Hoʻokuʻukuʻu ʻia e hele pōloli a hiki i ka wīwī loa ʻana o kona kino a kū maoli i ka nāwaliwali. Ua hele nā maka a hihia pūnāwelewele.

I kekahi pō, kolo aku nei ʻo ia a hiki i ka māla ʻuala a kekahi mau ʻele-mākule, a ma laila ia i nalinali ai i nā hua ʻuala i loaʻa aku iā ia. A no ka māluhiluhi no ka loa o ke ala āna i kolo mai ai, ua hāʻule iho nei ʻo ia e moe.

I ke kakahiaka ʻana aʻe, hele mai nei ka luahine i ka ʻeli ʻuala. I kona ʻike ʻana i ke okaoka o ka ʻuala i naunau ʻia, ua manaʻo ʻo ia ua komo ʻia ka māla ʻuala a lāua e ka honu, a kāhea aku nei i ka ʻelemakule, "E Pāpā ē! Hele mai kāua e huli i kēia honu i ʻai iho nei i ka ʻuala a kāua!" I ko lāua huli ʻana, loaʻa aku ʻo Keahiʻāloa e hiamoe ana. Nui ko lāua hauʻoli i ka loaʻa ʻana o kēia kaikamahine iā lāua, ʻoiai ʻaʻohe a lāua kama. Hoʻihoʻi aku nei lāua i ke kaikamahine i ka hale, a kapa iho nei i kona inoa ʻo Honu.

I ka nui ʻana o kēia kaikamahine, ua ʻike ʻia kona ʻano ʻeʻepa. Ua hiki iā ia ke kilo ʻōuli a ke haʻi ʻē aku i kona mau kahu hānai i nā mea e hiki mai ana. I nā wā a pau e piʻi mau ana kēia wahine ʻōpio i ke kuahiwi— ʻaʻole nō hoʻi i nele kona ʻohuʻohu i ka maile, lehua me ka mokihana i ka hoʻi ʻana mai. ʻO kekahi mea leʻaleʻa āna, ʻo ia nō ka heʻe hōlua ʻana me nā ʻōpio o ka ʻāina.

I kekahi lā, huli aku nei ʻo Keahiʻāloa i kona mau kahu hānai a ʻī aku nei, "E kupuna mā ē! Ua luhi ʻolua iaʻu, a ua ʻike ʻia maila au, ua wahine. E pono ʻo au ke luhi aku iā ʻolua. Inā ʻolua e hoʻolohe iaʻu, e ʻai aliʻi auaneʻi ʻolua! I ka lā ʻapōpō e hele kākou i ke kuahiwi i kalo a i ʻawa, a pau ia, e hele kākou i ke kahakai i nā ʻono like ʻole o ke kai. He malihini ana kā kākou e kiʻi mai ana iaʻu i wahine!"

Ma mua o ka piʻi ʻana mai o ka lā, ua piʻi aku nei lākou nei i ka uka no ka huhuki kalo a me ka ʻawa. Ma mua o ke kau ʻana o ka lā i ka lolo, ua puka lākou i ka hale. Hele nō hoʻi a ʻaui ka lā, ua moʻa ka ʻai a ua pau i ke kuʻi. Ua ʻaneʻane ka lā e napoʻo, ua hiki aku lākou i ke kahakai, a ʻaʻole nō hoʻi i ʻemo, ua lawa nā iʻa i makemake ʻia ai. I ka mākaukau ʻana o nā mea a pau, ʻī maila ke kaikamahine, "E hoʻi kākou e moe, a i kēia wanaʻao e hiki mai ai kuʻu malihini."

I ka wanaʻao ʻana aʻe, hiki ʻiʻo mai ana ka malihini—ʻo ke keiki a ke konohiki o ka ʻāina. Ua hele ʻo ia e nānā i nā loko iʻa a ke aliʻi, a i ka pōʻeleʻele loa ʻana, ua hūhewa ʻo ia. Kokoke e ao ka pō, i ka huli ia i ke alanui e hiki aku ai i kahi kamaʻāina, ʻaʻole i loaʻa. I ka hiki ʻana i kahi o nā ʻelemākule, ua haʻukeke i ke anu, a ua hele nō hoʻi a pōloli.

Ala mai nā ʻelemākule e hoʻokipa i ka malihini, a i ke kaikamahine nō hoʻi ka hoʻomākaukau ʻana i ka papa ʻaina nāna. I ka māʻona ʻana o ua keiki nei, nīnau mai nei i nā ʻelemākule, "ʻEa! Na ʻolua anei kēia kaikamahine?" "ʻAe, na māua nō." "Makemake akula kā hoʻi au i wahine naʻu. Pehea ko ʻolua manaʻo?" i nīnau hou mai ai ʻo ia. "Kā! ʻAʻole hoʻi no māua e hoʻāo aku ana. E noi aku nō ʻoe iā ia!"

I ka noi ʻia ʻana, ua hāʻawi koke maila nō ia i ka ʻae. Hele nō hoʻi a awakea, hoʻi aku nei ka ʻōpio e haʻi i nā mākua ua loaʻa kāna wahine. ʻO ko lākou hoʻomākaukau ihola nō ia i hale pili hou, i mau moena, kapa, a pēlā aku, no nā ʻōpio. A ua manaʻo ʻia aia a piha ke anahulu, kiʻi mai i ka wahine.

Iā Keahiʻāloa e noho ana ma Kauaʻi, ua hele maila kekahi kanaka i ka hale o nā mākua ponoʻī, a haʻi nō hoʻi i ka hoʻomāinoino ʻia o ke kaikamahine e ka makuahine makua, a i kahi lā ua ʻauana ua kaikamahine nei a nalowale. I ka lohe ʻana o ka makua kāne i kēia mea, pepehi ʻia e ia kāna wahine a ʻeha loa me ka nuku pū, "ʻAʻole naʻu i hāʻawi i kuʻu kaikamahine. Ma muli o kō paʻakikī, lilo kuʻu lei hoʻokahi i kō kaikuaʻana! ʻAlaʻala! E hana ʻoe i hoʻokahi kaʻau moena makaliʻi, hoʻokahi kaʻau moena pūʻao, a i hoʻokahi kaʻau paʻūpaʻū, a inā e paʻa ʻole iā ʻoe i ke anahulu hoʻokahi, pepehi hou ʻia ʻoe a ʻu a ʻeha loa!"

No ke aloha o ka ʻohana i ka wahine, hoʻokahi nō laulima ʻana i ka hana, a ma mua o ka piha ʻana o ke anahulu ua mākaukau nā mea a pau. ʻO ke kau nō ia o nā mākua i ka waʻa, a holo aku nei no Kauaʻi. Iā ia nei i ke ala, moe ʻuhane aku nei i ka ʻaumakua manō ona. ʻĪ mai nei ka ʻuhane o ua manō nei, "Ō hele! A 'o au pū me 'oe. 'O ka hale e kau 'ia ana e ka 'ōnohi, aia i laila ka lei a kāua." I ka puoho 'ana o kona hiamoe, ua ho'olana 'ia kona mana'o no ka 'ike hou 'ana i kāna mea aloha.

I ke kokoke 'ana i ka lā e ho'āo 'ia ai nā 'ōpio, 'ōlelo aku nei 'o Keahi-'āloa i nā 'elemākule, "I moe 'olua i kēia pō, a i lohe 'olua i ka hū, a me ka halulu, mai ala 'olua. Moe nō 'olua a hiki i ke kakahiaka." I kēlā pō, lohe nā 'elemākule i ka halulu nui, moe mālie nō lāua a ao. I ko lāua ala 'ana, 'ike aku nei lāua he 'elua mau hālau nunui i kūkulu 'ia ma kahi 'ao'ao o ka hale o lākou.

I ke ahiahi 'ana iho, 'ī hou maila nō ka hānai a lāua, "Inā 'olua e lohe i ka nakeke, me he mea lā e kālai lā'au 'ia ana, mai ala a'e nei 'olua." I ka pō 'ana iho, ua puoho ka hiamoe o nā 'elemākule i ka nakeke, me he mea lā he kinikini nā kānaka e kālai lā'au ana. I ke ala 'ana o lāua i ke kakahiaka, ua piha 'o mua o ka hale o lākou i ka 'umeke a me nā pā lā'au like 'ole. Kāhāhā ko lāua na'au i nā hana kupanaha a ka hānai a lāua. Hā'upu a'e nei, 'o nā hoa kā paha o kēia kaikamahine e hele mau nei i ke kuahiwi, 'o nā menehune. 'A'ole na'e lāua i ho'opuka i ko lāua mana'o i kā lāua hānai.

A pō hou nō, pāpā aku nei 'o Keahi'āloa i nā kahu hānai 'a'ole e ala mai ke lohe i ke kohākohā o nā kumu lā'au me he mea lā e hina ana, me ka 'u'ina o ka lā'au e 'oki'oki 'ia ana. Lohe nō nā 'elemākule i nā hana kuli like 'ole o waho, moe mālie lāua a ao. I ka hele 'ana mai i waho, e kū ana kekahi āhua wahie nui. 'A'ohe nō o lāua nīele wale aku i ka hānai, 'oiai ua 'ike a'ela nō lāua i nā hana ho'okalakupua.

E like nō me kāna hana mua i ke a'o i nā 'elemākule e moe mālie a ao, pēia nō i hana ai i ka uhi hou 'ana mai o ka pouli. I kēlā pō, lohe nā 'elemākule i ke kohākohā o nā pōhaku, me ka hohono 'uahi, 'a'ole na'e lāua i ho'okuli i ke kauoha o ke kaikamahine. I ka pi'i 'ana mai o ka lā, ua nalowale ke āhua wahie, a ua piha pono nā 'umeke i ka poi.

A pō hou nō, 'ī mai nei 'o Keahi'āloa, "I lohe 'olua i ka 'oē o ke kai, a nehe o ka 'ili'ili i kahaone, mai ala mai 'olua, e moe a ao, a ala mai 'olua." Nui ka 'oē o ke kai i kēlā pō, a ua nehe ka 'ili'ili me he mea lā he mea kaumaha e kaualakō 'ia ana; moe mālie nō nā kahu hānai a kakahiaka. 'Ike mai nei lāua i nā 'ono like 'ole o ke kai; ka 'opihi, ka wana, ka he'e, limu, hā'uke'uke, 'o ka i'a nō ho'i; ua pau i ka hana 'ia, a ua miko i ke kōpī 'ia.

Nānā a'e nei 'o Keahi'āloa i ke kai, a 'ōlelo mai nei i nā kahu hānai, "I kēia lā e hiki mai ai ke konohiki, ka wahine, ke keiki a lāua, me nā kānaka, no ka ho'āo 'ana iā māua. A i kēia lā pū nō ho'i e hō'ea mai ai ku'u mau mākua mai Hawai'i mai. I kū ka 'ōnohi i ka hale nei a i ka moana, 'ike iho kākou he pae wale mai nō i kula. 'O ka hālau ma 'ane'i, no ke konohiki, a 'o kēlā ma 'ō no ku'u mau mākua."

I ke kau pono 'ana o ka lā i ka lolo, ua hiki maila ke konohiki me kona 'ohana, me nā makana he nui. Iā lākou nō a noho, 'ula ana ka pūnohu ma luna o kaupoku hale. I ka 'ike 'ana o ka makua kāne i kāna lei ho'o-kahi, uē hāmama a'e nei 'o ia i ke aloha keiki—"'Auē ku'u lei, ku'u pua! Lawe 'ia mai kā 'oe i ka 'āina malihini e ho'omāinoino 'ia ai, e hele 'auana ai—kohu ao kuewa! Keahi'āloa ē! Ku'u kaikamahine 'alo i nā 'īnea he nui!"

'Akahi nō nā 'elemākule a 'ike 'o Keahi'āloa ka inoa o ke kaikamahine, a he pua ali'i kēia. 'O Honu wale nō ka inoa a lāua e hea ai.

Kūnānā ke konohiki o hō'ole nā mākua i ka ho'āo o nā keiki, akā, i ka ho'ākāka 'ana o Keahi'āloa i kona mālama maika'i 'ia e kēia mau 'ele-mākule, a no kona aloha nui iā lāua, ua hā'awi 'o ia i kona 'ae e lilo i hūnōna na ke konohiki. 'Ae nō nā mākua, 'o ka ho'āo 'ia nō ia o lāua i kēlā lā.

I ka pau 'ana o ka 'aha'aina, kū a'e nei 'o Keahi'āloa a kau kānāwai maila no kāna mau pulapula no ka wā pau 'ole. 'A'ole e hā'awi i ke keiki a ka muli na ka mua e hānai, o make. 'O ke keiki a ka mua na ka muli e luhi, ola. No laila ua mālama loa kāna mau pulapula i kēlā kānāwai a ko lākou kupuna, Keahi'āloa, a hiki i kēia lā.

The English-language version of this story, *The Story of Keahi'āloa*, appears on page 85.

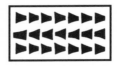

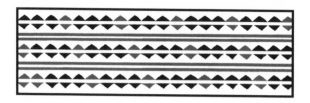

NĀ ʻŌLOHE O ʻŌLAʻA

He poʻe pōā nā ʻōlohe o ʻŌlaʻa. I loko o nā ana lākou i noho ai i loko o ka ulu lāʻau. Ke hele ka poe kaʻahele mai Kaʻū a Puna, mai Puna a Hilo, a mai Hilo a Kaʻū, ua pepehi ʻia lākou a make a lawe ʻia nā mea a pau mai ko lākou mau kino aku a hūnā ʻia.

Penei kā lākou hana ʻana. Ua piʻi aku kekahi o lākou i luna o ke kumu lāʻau a nānā i uka a i kai. Inā ʻaʻohe kanaka, kāhea aʻela ke kiu, "Kai a maloʻo," inā he kākaʻikahi loa nā kānaka e hele mai ana, kāhea aʻela ke kiu, "Kai make," inā he ʻumi paha a ʻoi iki, "Kai nui," a inā he nui loa, "Kai koʻo."

Ma kēia kāhea ʻana e maopopo ai ka heluna o nā poʻe e hele mai ana. Inā he ʻuʻuku, i ke alanui nō a make i ka pepehi ʻia; inā he nui iki, ua kono ʻia e hoʻi i ke ana e ʻai ai a e moe ai, a ke nanea, ua hāʻule mai nā pōhaku nunui i hoʻopaʻa ʻia ma luna o ko lākou wahi e nonoho ana, i luna o ko lākou mau poʻo, a make loa. ʻO ke "Kai koʻo," he hoʻokuʻu ʻia nō e hele i ko lākou alahele.

ʻO kekahi o nā ʻōlohe, ʻo Kapuaʻeuhi kona inoa. He ʻelua āna mau kaikamahine nunui ikaika, a ʻo lāua nō kona kōkua i loko o nā hana a pau. Ua aʻo ʻia kēia mau kaikamāhine i ka lua a me ka hakakā a ua like loa nō lāua me nā kāne. He mau mea akamai loa lāua i ka hoʻopunipuni hoʻopalai maka.

Oi hana aku kēia poʻe ʻōlohe pēia a make kekahi keiki o Kaʻū iā lākou. No ka minamina loa o ka ʻohana, ua hele ia e nīnau i ke kahuna i ka mea e hana ai, a ua kuhikuhi ʻia mai e hoʻouna i nā pōkiʻi hoa hānau e pepehi i kēlā ʻohana ʻōlohe.

Ua hele akula nā hoa hānau o ke kanaka i pepehi ʻia a i ka hiki ʻana aku i ʻŌlaʻa, ua hui aku nei me nā kaikamāhine a ka ʻōlohe a hoʻomaka aku nei e hakakā. ʻAneʻane nō hoʻi kekahi keiki e pōʻino, ʻo ka pahemo nō ia o kona malo a paʻa kekahi kihi i kona lima. Me kēia malo ʻo ia i hoʻohei aku ai i ka ʻāʻī o kēlā kaikamahine a ʻo kona ʻumi ʻia nō ia a make. 'O kona kōkua akula nō ia i kona hoa i ka pepehi 'ana i ka lua o ke kaikamahine. Ua lawe 'ia nā kino e hūnā a iho aku nei nā kānaka i loko o ke ana e kakali ai a ho'i mai ka makua kāne o ua mau kaikamāhine nei i pepehi 'ia e lāua.

I ka 'ike 'ana o ka 'elemakule i nā 'ōpio e nonoho mai ana i ka puka o ke ana, nīnau maila 'o ia, "'Auhea ku'u mau kaikamāhine?" "'Auhea lā? Hele a'e nei māua i ke ala a māluhiluhi a komo mai nei ma 'ane'i e ho'o-maha ai." "Komo mai ho'i hā ma loko nei," wahi a ka 'ōlohe. Leha aku nei nā keiki i luna a 'ike i ke kakau mai o nā pōhaku pepehi kanaka i luna a hō'ole aku nei, "'A'ole. Mahalo i kou lokomaika'i, ma 'ane'i nō māua e noho ai."

No'ono'o a'e nei ka 'elemakule ua pepehi 'ia nā kaikamāhine āna e kēia mau malihini, a 'o kona lele maila nō ia e pepehi iā lāua. 'Elua lāua lā, he mau kānaka 'ōpio, a ho'okahi nō kēia, he 'elemakule, a 'o ka hopena 'o ka make o ka 'ōlohe kolohe nui wale.

Ua 'ōlelo 'ia, aia nō nā mea a ka 'ōlohe i lawe kolohe ai i loko o ke ana o Kapua'euhi, akā, 'a'ohe po'e e ola nei i 'ike i nā pōhaku e uai ai e loa'a aku ai nā lua huna.

The English-language version of this story, *The Robbers of 'Ōla'a*, appears on page 91.

NĀ MAKAPŌ O MOAʻULA

No Moaʻula, Kaʻū, kekahi mau kānaka makapō. Hoʻokahi kanaka, ua makapō loa, a ʻo kekahi hoʻi, ua hiki nō ke ʻike iki i nā mea wale nō i kokoke loa i kona alo. Ua kūkā iho nei lāua e iho i Punaluʻu i kekahi lā, a na ke kanaka ʻike iki e alakaʻi i kona hoa makapō loa.

Ua iho mālie aku nei lāua a hiki ma ke kapa o Punaluʻu kahawai. Nīnau aku nei ka mea makapō loa i kona hoa,

"Pehea, he wai anei ko lalo?"

Pane maila kona hoa,

"ʻAe, he wai."

"Nui anei ka wai?"

"ʻAe, nui ka wai o lalo."

"A laila e lēkei aku kāua a ʻau aku no kēlā ʻaoʻao ma ʻō."

"ʻAe, e lēkei aʻe kāua."

Ua lēkei akula lāua i lalo, a hakihaki nā wāwae. He wai nō ko lalo, ʻaʻole naʻe he nui.

ʻAʻole nō kēia ka mea i pau ai ʻo ko lāua hele ʻana. I kekahi lā hele hou nō ua mau makapō nei i Punaluʻu kahawai, ma uka naʻe lāua i hele ai i kēia hanana. I ka hiki ʻana ma kahawai ua nīnau aku ka makapō mua i kona alakaʻi,

"Pehea kāu ʻike ʻana? Ua ʻuʻuku anei ka wai?"

"ʻAe ʻuʻuku loa."

"He mea ʻoiaʻiʻo anei kēnā, ʻaʻohe wai o lalo?"

"He ʻoiaʻiʻo, ʻaʻohe wai."

"E hele hoʻi hā kāua i lalo a hele wāwae aku ma ʻō."

A ua iho aku nei lāua i lalo.

ʻO ka mea a lāua i ʻike ai, ua piha ke kahawai i ka wai a lilo lāua. Ua ʻike ʻia lāua e kūpaka ana i loko o ka wai a kiʻi ʻia mai a hoʻihoʻi ʻia i uka. Pau loa nō ko lāua makemake ʻana e hele hou ma Punaluʻu me ka hele pū ʻole me ka poʻe maka ʻike.

The English-language version of this story, *The Blind Men of Moaʻula*, appears on page 93.

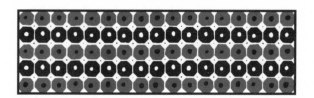

HĀMAMALAU

He wahine uʻi ʻo Hāmamalau, a ua kaulana ʻo ia mai kahi pae a kahi pae o ka ʻāina. Ua kiʻi ʻia mai ʻo ia i wahine na kekahi kanaka uʻi, a uʻi aʻe ʻo ia. Ma hope o ka hoʻāo ʻana ua hoʻi aku nei ʻo ia i ka ʻāina o kāna kāne.

No ka uʻi loa o Hāmamalau ua piha loa ke kāne i ka lili. Ua kūkulu ihola ʻo ia i hale ma luna pono o kekahi loko nui i ʻole ai e hiki i kāna wahine ke hele. Ke hoʻi mai ʻo ia, ma luna mai ia o kekahi waʻa ʻuʻuku e lawa pono ai nona hoʻokahi wale nō, a ke hele ʻo ia, ua hoʻopaʻa ʻia e ia ka puka a paʻa.

I kinohi, hele ke kāne a hoʻi mai i nā lā a pau, a ma hope mai hele noʻonoʻo ʻole ʻo ia i ka wahine e noho hoʻokahi ana i ka hale. Hele a pau ka malama, hoʻi mai me ka ʻai a me ka iʻa, a hele hou aku ana a hala ka malama, hoʻi mai ana. Pēlā ʻo ia i hana mau ai. ʻAi aʻela nō ka wahine a pau nā mea ʻai a ke kāne i hoʻolako mai ai a noho mālie nō e kakali a hoʻi hou mai ke kāne me kahi mea ʻai hou.

Oi kali mai ka ʻohana o Hāmamalau ʻo ka hoʻi aku hoʻi o ke kaikamahine e ʻike iā lākou a i ʻole hōʻike ʻia aku hoʻi no kona noho ʻana. No ko lākou noʻonoʻo nui loa, ua hoʻouna ʻia mai ka pōkiʻi kaikunāne e ʻike iā ia. I ka hele ʻana mai o ke kaikunāne, ua launa akula ʻo ia me kekahi mau hoa aloha o kona kaikoʻeke a lohe aʻe nei e pili ana no kona kaikuahine. Ua ʻike aʻela ke kaikunāne i ahonui nō ʻo Hāmamalau no ke aloha nō i ke kāne.

ʻAʻole ʻo ia i hele pololei aku i ka hale o kona hānau mua, akā, ua hoʻi akula ʻo ia me nā hoa aloha o ke kāne a Hāmamalau. I laila ʻo ia i hoʻolālā ai i kāna mea e hana ai i pakele kona kaikuahine.

I kekahi pō ua nui, ua kiʻi aʻe nei ʻo ia i kekahi waʻa a neʻe akula ma waho o ka puka o ka hale o kona kaikuahine. Ua pinana ua keiki ʻeu nei i luna o ka hale e hukihuki ai a hemohemo kekahi mau pili, a me ka maʻalahi loa ʻo ia i wehe ai i ka puka o ka hale a komo aku nei i loko.

Ua ʻike ʻo ia i ke kaikuahine e moe mai ana ma kūʻono, a hea aku nei, "E Hāmamalau ē! Ke kulu nei koʻu wahi. E neʻeneʻe mai." Kuhihewa a Hāmamalau ʻo ke kāne kēia e kāhea nei, a neʻeneʻe maila nō. Ua neʻe akula ke kaikunāne a kāhea hou nō, "E Hāmamalau ē! Ke kulu nei koʻu wahi, neʻeneʻe mai."

Pēlā lāua i neʻe ai a hiki i ka puka o ka hale, a ʻo ka hehi akula nō ia o ke kaikunāne i luna o kona waʻa. He pō pouli ia, ʻaʻohe i ʻike ʻia nā hōkū e kau ana, a no laila ua manaʻo nō ʻo Hāmamalau aia nō ʻo ia i loko o ka hale. I ka neʻe hou ʻana aku ona, ʻo kona kau pono nō ia i luna o ka waʻa o ke kaikunāne. Me ka ʻāwīwī i hoe ai ke kaikunāne a ka mākāhā a hāpai i ka waʻa o lāua a hāʻule ma waho a ʻo ka holo loa akula nō ia o lāua no ko lāua one hānau.

I ka ʻike ʻana o nā mākua iā Hāmamalau, ua nui ko lāua aloha. ʻO kēia wahine uʻi, ua hele a wīwī ʻino a poʻopoʻo nā maka. ʻO ma laila lāua i hoʻohiki ai ʻaʻole e hoʻokuʻu hou i ke kaikamahine e hoʻi hou me ke kāne aloha ʻole.

Ua hoʻi aku ke kāne i ka hale a ʻike ua lilo ka wahine. Ua lohe ʻo ia ua kiʻi ʻia mai e ke kaikunāne e hoʻihoʻi, a ua ʻike nō hoʻi ʻo ia inā ʻo ia e kiʻi hou aku ana, e kipaku ʻia ana ʻo ia no ka hoʻomāinoino iā Hāmamalau. Pū aʻela nō kona manaʻolana no ka hele ʻana aku i mua o kāna wahine a no laila ua ʻimi hou akula ʻo ia i wahine nāna.

The English-language version of this story, *Hāmamalau, Open Leaf,* appears on page 94.

KALUAKOKO

I ka wā kahiko, ua noho kekahi kanaka me kāna wahine ma kēlā wahi e kapa 'ia nei 'o Reid's Bay. He kanaka lawai'a ia, a i nā lā mālie a pau ua hele 'o ia me kona wa'a i kāna hana ma'a mau. Ma hope iho, ua hui 'o ia me kekahi wahine no Keaukaha, a komo nō ho'i ka ho'ohihi o kekahi i kekahi. 'A'ole i huhū kāna wahine ho'āo i kona lohe 'ana i kēia mea, a ua kauoha aku nei i ke kāne, ke nui ho'i kāna i'a, e hā'awi i kekahi i kēlā wahine āna. Pēlā lākou i hana ai no kekahi mau makahiki.

I kekahi lā, huli aku nei ke kāne i kāna wahine a 'ī aku nei, "E ku'u wahine aloha ē, ua no'ono'o au he mea pono iā kākou me kō punalua e noho like, ma mua ho'i o ko'u hele 'ana i ka lawai'a a lawe aku i kona māhele iā ia, a 'o kā kāua iā kāua iho nō." Pane aku nei ka wahine, "He aha a'e nei ho'i ka pilikia o ia. Ō ki'i 'ia ku'u punalua a ho'iho'i mai, a noho like nō ho'i kākou." Ua ki'i 'ia ka wahine i Keaukaha a ho'iho'i 'ia mai a noho pū lākou.

'O ka mea 'ano 'ē i 'ike 'ia, 'o ia nō ka lili o ka wahine hou i ka wahine mua ke pili aku me ke kāne a lāua, 'a'ole na'e 'o ia i hō'ike a maka loa i kona mana'o inaina. I kekahi lā, ma mua o ka hele 'ana o ke kāne e lawai'a, ua pāpā 'o ia i nā wāhine 'a'ole e hele i ka lawai'a a ho'i mai 'o ia.

I ka wa'a nō a hala aku, koi aku nei ka wahine hou i kona kōko'olua, "E ia nei ē, ua nui maila paha nā pua i'a o kahakai, e hele kāua e kā'e'e pua." Pane maila kahi o lāua, "'A'ole; ua pāpā iho nei ke kāne a kāua i ka lawai'a. E noho nō kāua i ka hale nei." "Inā pēlā, hele a'e nō kāua ma kai nei e kā'e'e 'ōpae ai a ho'i mai." No ke koi pa'akikī loa o ka punalua, 'o kona 'ae akula nō ia, a hele aku nei lāua e kā'e'e 'ōpae.

Ua nanea loa ka wahine mua i ke kā'e'e 'ōpae a kokoke loa aku nei i ka waha o ka lua. Me ka hikiwawe loa ka punalua i 'onou ai iā ia ma hope mai a poholo 'o ia i loko o ka lua. Ua pani 'ia mai i ka pōhaku i hiki hou 'ole ai iā ia ke hemo i waho. Ma laila 'o ia a make loa. Ua ho'i aku ka wahine hou i ka hale me ka ho'iho'i 'ole i nā 'ōpae a lāua me ka 'upena kā'e'e o 'ike 'ia 'o ia kekahi i hele i kahakai.

I ka make ʻana o kēlā wahine, ua puka mai ke koko mai kona waha mai a hele aku nei i loko o ka huʻa kai a kahi a ke kāne e lawaiʻa ana, a hoʻomaka aʻe nei e kaʻapuni i ka waʻa. I ka ʻike ʻana o ke kāne i ka ʻāweʻaweʻa koko, ua hāʻupu aʻela ʻo ia i kāna wahine a hoʻopau i kāna lawaiʻa ʻana. Iā ia nō a hoʻohuli i ka waʻa, ʻo ke kaʻa nō ia o ke koko ma mua pono a alakaʻi aku nei i ka waʻa a kokoke i ka lua. Ua neʻe aku nei nō ke koko a ka waha o ka lua a komo aku nei i loko. I ka wehe ʻana mai o ke kāne i ka pani pōhaku, ua loaʻa aku ke kino make o kāna wahine.

Ua hāpai mai ʻo ia a kahi kokoke i ko lākou hale a hūnā ihola. Ua ʻike akula ʻo ia i kekahi wahine āna e kū mai ana i ka puka o ka hale. Nīnau aku nei ʻo ia, "ʻAuhea hoʻi kahi o ʻolua?" Pane mai nei ka wahine, "ʻAʻole au i ʻike. Koi mai nei iaʻu e hele me ia i ke kāʻeʻe ʻōpae, a no koʻu ʻae ʻole ʻana e hele, hele hoʻokahi aku nei me ka ʻupena kāʻeʻe. ʻAʻole nō i hoʻi mai nei."

Ua piha loa ke kāne i ka huhū. ʻĪ aku nei ʻo ia, "He wahine hoʻopunipuni ʻoe! Nāu i pepehi a make kaʻu wahine aloha! Ua nui koʻu aloha iā ia. Iaʻu e lawaiʻa ana ua kiʻi aʻe nei kona koko iaʻu e hoʻi mai." I kēlā manawa nō ua pepehi ʻia ʻo ia a make e ke kāne. A lawe loa akula ke kāne i ka wahine mua e hoʻonalo i ka lua pao. ʻO ka lua o ka wahine, na kona ʻohana nō i kiʻi mai a hoʻonalo aku. Pau ka hoʻi hou ʻana mai o ia kanaka e noho hou ma laila. No kēia kumu i hea ʻia ai kēlā lua ʻo Kaluakoko.

The English-language version of this story, *The Hole of Blood*, appears on page 95.

KA U'I PALAUALELO

I kekahi lā ua hele aku nei kekahi mau kaikamāhine i ka 'eli 'uala. A pau ka 'eli 'ana, ua lawe aku nei lāua i nā 'uala a lāua ma lalo o ke kumu pūhala e pūlehu ai. Ma hope o ka 'ā 'ana o kā lāua mau ahi, ua 'ō'ili mai ka ipo a kekahi o lāua. I ia manawa, pi'i aku nei lāua i luna o ke kumu pūhala e ho'oipoipo ai.

I kēlā a me kēia manawa, ua kāhea ke kaikamahine i luna o ka pūhala i ko lalo kaikamahine, "'Ea, e ho'ohulihuli a'e 'oe i ku'u 'uala." "'Ae," wahi a ke kaikamahine ma lalo, a ho'ohuli a'e nei i kāna 'uala pono'ī me ka nānā 'ole i kā kekahi o lāua. A mo'a kekahi 'uala, pau nō i ka 'ai 'ia e ia, a pūlehu hou nō i 'uala nāna. Kāhea hou nō ke kaikamahine o luna, "E ho'ohuli a'e 'oe i ku'u 'uala." Pane nō ke kaikamahine e pūlehu 'uala ana, "'Ae." Hele iho nei a pau kā ia nei 'uala, 'o ko ia nei hele nō ia i ka 'au'au kai.

Noho iho nei ke kaikamahine o luna o ka pūhala a hā'upu i kāna 'uala, kāhea hou nō, "E ia nei, e ho'ohuli mai ho'i 'oe i ku'u 'uala." 'A'ohe pane i loa'a aku iā ia. Kāhea hou a'e nei me ka leo nui, "E ho'ohuli a'e ho'i 'oe i ku'u 'uala!" 'A'ohe nō he pane. 'O ko lāua iho maila nō ia i lalo.

Ua pau ka 'uala a kekahi kaikamahine, ua mo'a a ua pau i ka 'ai. 'O kā kēia kaikamahine ho'i, ua pāpa'a ka 'uala i kapuahi, a 'o ka nui 'uala, e maka ana nō. Ua pi'i kona huhū i kona hoa a i ka ho'i 'ana mai o kēlā kaikamahine mai ka 'au'au kai mai, ua noke akula 'o ia i ka nuku.

Me ka mino'aka i pane 'ia mai ai 'o ia, "'A'ohe u'i palaualelo o Ka'ū." A me kēia mau hua 'ōlelo ua kū akula 'o ia a hele me ka ipo a kona hoa. Ua 'ike kēlā kanaka, inā 'o ka u'i palaualelo kāna wahine, e pāpa'a ana ka 'uala i kapuahi.

The English-language version of this story, *The Lazy Beauty*, appears on page 99.

Pāʻūohiʻiaka

KAWELOHEA

He wahine kaulana 'o Kawelo i ka u'i, mai kahi pae a kahi pae o Ka'ū. No ka u'i loa o kēia wahine, ua lili loa kāna kāne iā ia. He huhū ia ke launa aku me nā kānaka o ka 'āina.

I kekahi lā, i ka 'ike 'ana o ke kāne iā ia e kama'ilio ana me kekahi o ko lāua makamaka, ua pi'i loa kona inaina, a ua pepehi 'ia 'o Kawelo a make loa. Ho'iho'i 'ia ke kino wailua i loko o ka lua pao i ka lae kahakai. I nā lā a pau a ke kāne e hele ana i ka lawai'a, e hea mau ana ka leo o Kawelo mai ke ana mai:

> E ku'u kāne ē,
> Aloha 'ole 'oe ia'u!
> 'A'ohe kā 'oe e ki'i mai ia'u
> E hele pū nō kāua i ka lawai'a!
> Ku'u kāne aloha 'ole ē!

E nele mau ana nō ho'i ke kāne i ka i'a. A no kona uluhua a ho'onāukiuki i ka hea mau 'ia, ki'i aku nei i ka iwi o ka wahine. Lawe aku nei, a ma ke kapa o kekahi puhi, ku'iku'i 'ia ka iwi a okaoka, me ka namunamu pū nō: "I kū kā ho'i kāu kāhea pinepine i ka okaoka 'ole o kō iwi. Eia mai!" A pau kāna ku'i i nā iwi, waiho 'ia nō ma kahi i wāwahi 'ia ai. Pā nō ka lā i ua āhua iwi nei, a kuakea. I ka pi'i 'ana o ke kai mai loko mai o ke puhi, ua holoi 'ia ua mau iwi nei a lilo i lalo. I nā manawa a pau e hea mau ana kona leo mai loko mai o ke puhi:

> Ku'u kāne aloha 'ole ē!
> E ki'i mai 'oe ia'u e hele pū me 'oe!

'A'ole hiki i ke kāne ke ki'i aku, 'oiai he make wale nō kona ke komo i loko o ua puhi nei. Ho'okahi nō mea pono, 'o ka 'u'umi i ka huhū.

Pēia kēia wahine i hea ai a hiki i ka make 'ana o ke kāne āna. Ma hope mai o ia manawa, aia nō ka hea o Kawelo a he mea 'ano nui e hiki mai ana ma luna o ka ʻāina. No laila ua lilo kēia puhi i mea wānana i nā kamaʻāina o ia wahi. I ka wā o Kamehameha e noho aliʻi ana, ua hea hou mai ʻo Kawelo mai loko o ke puhi, "No ka ʻāina ʻē ka ʻāina! No ka ʻāina ʻē ka ʻāina!" Hea maila nō hoʻi kānaka mai luna mai, "E Kawelo ē! No Kamehameha ka ʻāina. No Paiʻea ʻo Hawaiʻi nei!" Pane maila nō ka leo—"ʻAʻole! ʻAʻohe no Paiʻea ka ʻāina; no ke kai ka ʻāina! No ka ʻāina ʻē ka ʻāina!" Lohe ʻia kona leo mai Paepae mai, kahi o ua lua nei (ma lalo pono o ka pali Pōhina), mai Pāhala a Kahuku. Lilo nō hoʻi kēia i mea nui na kānaka o ia wahi e kūkā kamaʻilio ai.

ʻAʻole i pau kāna hea ʻana a hiki i ka hoʻohui ʻia ʻana o ka ʻāina nei me ʻAmelika Huipū. Ma hope o ka make ʻana o Kamehameha, ua hoʻomau nō ʻo ia i ka hea, "No ka ʻāina ʻē ka ʻāina!" Ua ʻōlelo ʻia e kamaʻāina o ia wahi, i ka hoʻolālā ʻia ʻana e hoʻohui i ka ʻāina me ʻAmelika, ua wānana mua ʻia ia mea e Kawelo, ma ka hea ʻana, "E kuʻu lāhui ē! Hoʻohui ʻāina! Hoʻohui ʻāina! No ka ʻāina ʻē ka ʻāina!"

I kekahi lā, ua hele kekahi poʻe i ka lae kahakai, a ua ʻupu aʻela nō hoʻi ka manaʻo kolohe i loko o lākou; wāwahi ʻia ka waha o ua puhi nei a hāmama loa. (Hiki ʻole nō hoʻi ke waiho mālie i nā mea maikaʻi a ke akua i hana ai!) Ua hea hou nō ʻo Kawelo, akā, no ka hāmama loa o luna, ʻaʻole puka mōakāka ʻo ka hua ʻōlelo. ʻO ka poʻe kokoke loa wale nō ka poʻe maopopo i ka mea e ʻōlelo ʻia ana. ʻO ka leo wale nō kā ka poʻe mamao iki, ke lohe, a ʻo ka hua ʻōlelo hoʻi, palalē loa.

No kona hea mau, ua kapa ʻia kēlā puhi, "ʻO ka puhi o Kawelohea."

The English-language version of this story, *Kawelo the Shouter,* appears on page 100.

KALĀKOLOHE

'O Kalākolohe kekahi kahuna kaulana o Ka'ū. 'A'ole 'o ia he kahuna kinai ola; he kahuna lapa'au 'o ia, he kilo 'ōuli, a 'o Lā kekahi o kona mau akua. Aia i ke awāwa 'o Honokāne ka heiau i mālama 'ia e kona mau kūpuna a hiki i ka manawa i ho'opau loa 'ia ai 'o ia mau mea.

'O Mr. Hutchinson ke po'o nui o ka mahi kō 'o Hutchinson Sugar Plantation Company i ka wā e ola ana 'o Kalākolohe. I nā Hawai'i o Ka'ū, 'o "Palapoi" wale nō ka inoa o Mr. Hutchinson. 'O ke kumu i hea 'ia ai 'o Palapoi, no ka pāpa'a lā o ka 'ā'ī, a 'āka'aka'a mai ka 'ili e like me ka poi malo'o.

Ua lohe pinepine 'o Mr. Hutchinson i ka mana o Kalākolohe, he hiki wale nō ke ho'okō 'ia mai nā mea āna e pule aku ai, a no laila i ka malo'o 'ana o ka 'āina i ka ua 'ole, ua hele akula 'o ia e nonoi i ka 'olu'olu o Kalākolohe e pule i ua. Ua pule 'o Kalākolohe, a ua helele'i mai ka ua e lawa maika'i ai nō no nā mea ulu. I ka malo'o hou 'ana nō o nā kō a me ka mau'u o ke kula, ua iho hou nō 'o Mr. Hutchinson iā Kalākolohe e pule i ua. Ua ho'okō 'ia nō kona makemake.

No ka hele pinepine aku o kēia haole iā Kalākolohe e pule i ua, ua piha 'o ia i ka uluhua, a pule aku nei i ua nui. I ka pō a me ka lā i ua 'ia ai no kekahi mau pule a hiki i ka hele 'ana o Hutchinson e noi e ho'opau 'ia ka ua.

'O ka ho'i hou 'ana mai o ke kau wela, ua 'ula pū nā 'āina kula i ka mau'u malo'o. 'A'ohe lawa ka holoholona i ka wai e inu ai. Ho'i hou akula nō 'o Hutchinson iā Kalākolohe e noi e hā'awi 'ia mai i ua. E like nō me ma mua i ka hana mao 'ole o ka ua, pēlā nō i kēia hanana, a hiki i ka noi hou 'ana o ka haole e ho'opau. Pēlā i hana 'ia ai no kekahi mana-wa lō'ihi.

Ho'okahi lā, ua iho mai 'o Hutchinson e noi i ua iā Kalākolohe. Ua hele kēia kahuna a uluhua maoli a nīnau aku nei,

"E Palapoi, ua nui anei kou makemake i ua?"

"'Ae, ua nui ko'u makemake i ua, ke malo'o maila ke kō."

"Inā 'oe e makemake loa i ka ua, e ki'i 'oe i kō pū a kī i ke papakole o ka lā."

A me kēia mau hua 'ōlelo ua kū aku nei 'o Kalākolohe a ho'i i loko o kona hale me ka nānā hou 'ole mai i ka haole e kū nei ma waho me ke 'ano hoka.

I kēlā pō, iā Kalākolohe e hiamoe ana, ua loa'a iā ia ka hō'ike e pōkole ana kona ola no kāna mau 'ōlelo ho'okano e kī i ke papakole o kona akua, o Lā. Ua ala a'e nei 'o ia a ho'āla i kona 'ohana a hō'ike aku nei iā lākou e make ana 'o ia no kāna mau 'ōlelo pono 'ole i kona akua. I ke ao 'ana a'e, ua lohe 'ia 'o Kalākolohe, ua make. Nui ka po'e o Ka'ū i hele e 'ike i ko lākou kahuna nui.

'O ka heiau o Honokāne, ua pau, akā, ke waiho lā nā pōhaku o ke kahua. Ua 'ōlelo 'ia i kahi wā, ke lohe 'ia nei nō ka wawā o ka leo oli, o ka wala'au i loko o ua awāwa nei, akā, 'a'ohe kanaka e 'ike 'ia ma laila. I loko o kēlā awāwa ua ulu wale ke kukui, noni, manakō, 'alani, hau, niu, hala, piku a me kekahi mau kumu lā'au 'ē a'e. Mai kahiko mai a hiki i ka wā e ola ana 'o Kalākolohe, he awāwa kapu kēia, a i kona make 'ana aku, he wahi hele 'ia e nā lāhui like 'ole, e ki'i e like me ka makemake i nā hua 'ai e ulu lā ma laila.

The English-language version of this story, *The Mischievous Sun,* appears on page 103.

REFERENCES

Alexander, W. D. *A Brief History of the Hawaiian People.* New York: (n.p.), 1891.

Beckwith, Martha Warren. "The Hawaiian Romance of Laieikawai" [by S. N. Haleole, 1863]. Thirty-third Annual Report of the Bureau of American Ethnology to the Secretary of the Smithsonian Institution, 1911–12. Washington, D.C.: Government Printing Office, 1919.

Beckwith, Martha Warren. *Kepelino's Traditions of Hawaii.* Bishop Museum Bulletin 95. Honolulu: Bishop Museum Press, 1932.

Brigham, William T. *Ka Hana Kapa: The Making of Bark-Cloth in Hawaii.* Bishop Museum Memoir 3. Honolulu: Bishop Museum Press, 1911.

Dibble, Sheldon. *History of the Sandwich Islands.* Lahainaluna: Press of the Mission Seminary, 1843.

Emerson, Joseph S. *Hawaiian String Games,* ed. Martha Warren Beckwith. Publications of the Folklore Foundations 5. Poughkeepsie, N.Y.: Vassar College, 1924.

Emerson, Joseph S. "Selections from a Kahuna's Book of Prayers," a paper read before the Hawaiian Historical Society in 1917 and published in *Hawaiian Historical Society Annual Report* 26, 1918.

Emerson, Nathaniel B. "Long Voyages of the Ancient Hawaiians," a paper read before the Hawaiian Historical Society, May 18, 1893, and published as no. 5 of the papers of the Society.

Fornander, Abraham. *An Account of the Polynesian Race.* Vol. 2. London: Trubner, 1878–80.

Fornander, Abraham. *Fornander Collection of Hawaiian Antiquities and Folk-Lore.* Bishop Museum Memoirs, vols. 4–6. Honolulu: Bishop Museum Press, 1916–20.

Grey, Sir George. *Polynesian Mythology and Ancient Traditional History of the New Zealand Race, as Furnished by Their Chiefs and Priests.* 2nd edn. Auckland: (n.p.), 1885.

Grey, Sir George. *Polynesian Mythology and Maori Legends.* London: (n.p.), 1885.

Handy, E.S.C. *Marquesan Legends.* Bishop Museum Bulletin 69. Honolulu: Bishop Museum Press, 1930.

Handy, E.S.C., and E. G. Handy. *Native Planters in Old Hawaii.* Bishop Museum Bulletin 233. Honolulu: Bishop Museum Press, 1972.

Kalakaua. *The Legends and Myths of Hawaii,* ed. R. M. Daggett. New York: Charles L. Webster, 1888.

Kūkahi, Joseph L. *Ke Kumulipo: He Moolelo Hawaii.* Honolulu, T.H.: Grieve Publishers, 1902.

Malo, David. *Hawaiian Antiquities (Moolelo Hawaii),* trans. by Nathaniel B. Emerson (1898). Honolulu: Hawaiian Gazette, 1903.

159

Pope, Katherine. *Hawaii, The Rainbow Land.* New York: Thomas Y. Crowell, 1924.

Pukui, Mary Kawena. *ʻŌlelo Noʻeau: Hawaiian Proverbs and Poetical Sayings.* Honolulu: Bishop Museum Press, 1983.

Pukui, Mary Kawena, and Samuel H. Elbert. *Hawaiian-English Dictionary.* Honolulu: University of Hawaii Press, 1957.

Pukui, Mary Kawena, *Hawaiian Dictionary.* Honolulu: University of Hawaii Press, 1971.

Pukui, Mary Kawena, *Hawaiian Grammar.* Honolulu: University Press of Hawaii, 1979.

Pukui, Mary Kawena, and E. S. Craighill Handy. *The Polynesian Family System in Ka-ʻu, Hawaiʻi.* Rutland, Vermont: Charles E. Tuttle, 1958.

Pukui, Mary Kawena, and Alfons L. Korn. *The Echo of Our Song: Chants and Poems of the Hawaiians.* Honolulu: University Press of Hawaii, 1973.

Pukui, Mary Kawena, Dorothy B. Barrère, and Marion Kelly. *Hula: Historical Perspectives.* Department of Anthropology, Pacific Anthropological Records 30. Honolulu: Bishop Museum Press, 1980.

Pukui, Mary Kawena, Samuel H. Elbert, and Esther T. Mookini. *Place Names of Hawaii.* Honolulu: University of Hawaii Press, 1974.

Pukui, Mary Kawena, E. W. Haertig, and Catherine A. Lee. *Nānā i ke Kumu (Look to the Source).* Honolulu: Hui Hānai, Queen Liliuokalani Children's Center, 1972.

Rice, W. H. *Hawaiian Legends.* Bishop Museum Bulletin 3. Honolulu: Bishop Museum Press, 1923.

Rock, Joseph F. *Indigenous Trees of the Hawaiian Islands.* Lāwai, Hawaiʻi: Pacific Tropical Botanical Garden, 1974.

Somadeva, Bhatta, with C. H. Tawney. *Katha Sarit Sagara,* or *Ocean of the Streams of Story.* 2d edn. Delhi: Munshiram Manoharlal, 1968.

Thrum, Thomas G. *Hawaiian Folk Tales.* Chicago: McClurg, 1921.

Thrum, Thomas G. *More Hawaiian Folk Tales.* Chicago: McClurg, 1923.

Westervelt, W. D. *Hawaiian Legends of Ghosts and Ghost-Gods.* Rutland, Vermont: Charles E. Tuttle, 1963.

Westervelt, W. D. *Hawaiian Legends of Old Honolulu.* Rutland, Vermont: Charles E. Tuttle, 1963.